Published by:
FPMI Communications, Inc.
707 Fiber St.
Huntsville, AL 35801-5833

(256) 539-1850
Fax: (256) 539-0911

Internet Address:
http://www.fpmi.com
e-mail: fpmi@fpmi.com

by G. Jerry Shaw and
Thomas J. O'Rourke

Table of Contents

Acknowledgements

The authors wish to extend their heartfelt appreciation to all of the individuals who contributed their time and talents to this project. Special thanks to Margaret P. Crenshaw for her steady encouragement in convincing the authors to undertake this venture.

G. Jerry Shaw
Thomas J. O'Rourke

Foreword

In ten years of working as a federal employee and over fifteen years in private practice representing federal employees, I have noticed that public employees share one common trait: their interest in their retirement program. Because of this, a book addressing wills, trusts, and estate planning, specifically designed for government employees, is an important aid to their retirement planning.

Many of us dream of a long and happy retirement... where the weather is good and the cost of living is reasonable.

Many of us dream of a long and happy retirement in a part of the world where the weather is good and the cost of living is reasonable. We don't stop to think that we need to make provisions for our loved ones, nor do we recognize the consequences of what may befall them if we fail to do so. This book is designed to take the "mystery" out of the terms and concepts we may find difficult, but which all of us must confront to protect our property and our families as we approach or reach retirement.

We hope that this book will help you better understand wills, trusts, and estates, and we hope that once you understand the estate planning process, you will take the steps necessary to protect yourself, your spouse and children, your grandchildren, and other loved ones.

Most of all, we hope that once you have done so, you will then have the peace of mind which will assure you a truly happy retirement after your many years of public service. Thanks for all you have done and are doing for our nation. We all gratefully appreciate your years of public service.

G. Jerry Shaw

Introduction

Government employees at the federal, state, and local levels do not as a group, earn enough money to "get rich" on their salaries. Most of them probably consider themselves underpaid and most probably think that they do not need estate planning.

If they purchase real estate in an appreciating market, however, have inherited or will inherit assets from elderly family members, and maximize investment opportunities offered during their careers, such as investing in the federal Thrift Savings Plan, they may well accumulate sufficient assets to make estate planning advisable.

Since government retirement programs often allow their employees to retire before age 62, government employees can collect their government retirement benefits and then begin second careers or take second jobs during their mid-to-late fifties.

After retiring from the government, many people begin second careers or take second jobs during their mid-to-late fifties.

This, plus the fact that family expenses such as home mortgage payments and children's educational expenses often cease during the same years, offers an opportunity for government workers to increase their financial holdings late in life. It also means that retirement planning and second career planning should include both financial and estate planning.

The first edition of this publication was prepared in response to numerous inquiries from government employee clients and other persons who had read articles on estate planning published in various periodicals.

It addressed the concerns faced by middle-income individuals in determining how to provide for their loved ones upon their death through the most effective use of the assets they accumulated during their careers in public service. Its intent is to provide general information and guidance to the layman, but it does not give definite guidance regarding estate, trust, or tax law. It is hoped that this book succeeds in making a complex area of the law somewhat more understandable.

Later editions have been expanded and up-dated in response to comments received from readers of the first and second editions, including new chapters on "How To Avoid Probate," "Your Net Worth For Estate Planning Purposes," "Planning For Long-Term Care," and "Tax-Favored Estate Accumulation Techniques." In addition, a more detailed discussion of two provisions of the Social Security laws affecting government retirees, the government pension offset and the windfall elimination provision, has been added.

This book is not a tax publication. Due to the pervasive effects of the tax law on all aspects of life, however, it does include a general discussion of the tax implications of estate, gift and trust transactions. The passage of the Tax Reform Act of 1976 implemented a major reform in estate and gift tax law. One of the purposes of this reform was to make only those individuals who had a gross estate in excess of $600,000 subject to estate and gift taxes. As a result, in 1976, a relatively small segment of the U.S. population needed to be concerned with these taxes. In 1976, however, it was possible to buy a comfortable, three-bedroom suburban house for $35,000 and a gallon of gasoline for $.50. With inflation, the increasing prevalence of two-income families, and the common use of life insurance, many middle-income individuals now face the possibility that a substantial portion of their assets may have to be paid in estate taxes at the time of death.

Because of this, the book includes a discussion of estate and gift tax laws and the various types of trusts which an individual can use to reduce the effect of these laws.

The chapters relating to wills, probate, revocable living trusts, living wills, durable powers of attorney, practical alternatives for gifts to children, how to avoid probate, planning for long-term-care, and tax-favored estate planning techniques are generally applicable to all persons, regardless of their financial status. The remaining chapters in this book relate to concerns of individuals who have estates in excess of $600,000.

At various intervals in the text the authors have inserted a "Case in Point" to provide readers with true-to-life examples which illustrate that some of the technical principles and terms explained in the text may play a very practical role in their lives.

Readers may be unfamiliar with many of the terms which appear throughout the text. In an effort to make this material as clear as possible, the authors have underlined technical terms when such terms initially appear. Any term which is underlined is defined in the Glossary at the end of this book.

For the sake of simplicity the authors have frequently employed the male gender when using pronouns. Because the authors are fully aware of women's changing roles in society as a whole, this purely editorial decision is intended as neither a deliberate nor inadvertent social misstatement.

Finally, this publication is not intended to be a definitive treatise on estate, gift, or tax law. It does not address such matters as generation skipping taxes and the applicability of state and local taxes to a given individual. It is intended to provide general guidance and should not be relied upon as a substitute for the advice of a competent professional. Rather, it should prove to be a helpful complement to any such professional assistance.

CHAPTER 1

The Importance of Careful Estate Planning

The Importance of Careful Estate Planning

"Anyone who owns property or has a dollar that he doesn't plan to spend has an 'estate'. The state and federal government may have something to say about what he can do with it. But no other person can tell him what he is to do with that property, whether he is to keep it, sell it, exchange it or give it away. No one can tell him what he's to do with the dollar, whether he's to put it away in a savings account, what the form of the account should be or whatever. He alone can plan the estate."[1]

What is Estate Planning and What are its Benefits?

There are many advantages to planning carefully for the disposition of one's assets both during life and death.

An <u>estate plan</u> is nothing more than a formal plan for implementing an individual's wishes about what to do with property acquired during life. There are many advantages to planning carefully for the disposition of one's assets both during life and after death. They range from tax savings to the most basic desire to ensure that one's property is left to the intended beneficiaries. Careful estate planning can also ensure that disabled, young or elderly loved ones are adequately cared for under a variety of circumstances.

The preparation of an estate plan generally involves the preparation of a <u>will.</u> It may also include one or more trusts. Various chapters in this book also discuss the tax implications of estate planning, including the use of <u>powers of attorney, living wills, revocable living trusts, irrevocable trusts, life insurance trusts</u> and other considerations relevant to the planning of an estate.

---

[1] Kess and Westlin, *Estate Planning Guide*, Commerce Clearing House at p. 3 (1987 ed.)

What Property is Included in an Estate?

Before an individual can construct a plan for the management and disposition of his assets, he must first determine the nature and extent of his ownership interest in the assets. The type of property a person owns and the manner in which he holds title to the property play a vital role. A basic understanding of the consequences of various forms of property ownership is essential.

A basic understanding of the consequences of various forms of property ownership is essential.

Not All Property Passes Under a Will

Although a will prescribes how a deceased individual's property (money, real estate, personal possessions) will be distributed after death, certain types of property may pass outside of a will. Two common examples are items of property which pass at the time of death either by contract or by operation of law. By operation of law is a legal term which means that the law dictates that an event will occur, or that certain rights may be asserted or enforced upon the occurrence of a specific event regardless of the wishes of the party.

Life insurance is the most common example of property that passes by contract. A life insurance policy is a contract between the owner of the policy and the insurer. When the insured dies, the insurer is contractually obligated to pay any proceeds to the person named as the "designated beneficiary" (i.e., the person to whom the insurance proceeds are to be paid.)

Jointly Owned Property

Property that passes by operation of law includes certain jointly owned property. Title to property owned by two individuals may be held in one of three ways: as <u>tenants in common,</u> as <u>joint tenants with a right of survivorship,</u> or as <u>tenants by the entirety.</u>

In a <u>tenancy in common,</u> each tenant owns an undivided interest in the property. There is no right of survivorship and this interest may be passed to an individual in a will. The surviving owner, commonly referred to as "tenant," does not automatically receive the ownership interest of the decedent (i.e., the person who has died.) The term "undivided interest" is a technical legal term used in property law which means that each owner of a jointly held parcel of property has an equal right to use and enjoy any portion of the entire property. Thus, if Frances and Ruth own a mountain lot as tenants in common, each has equal rights of access to the entire lot. Neither may restrict the other's right to use any portion of the entire lot. If Frances owns a 75 percent interest in the lot and Ruth owns the remaining 25 percent, each is entitled to a proportionate share of any proceeds when the lot is sold. Ruth, however, has equal rights to use and possess the entire lot as long as she and Frances own it as tenants in common.

As joint tenants with the right of survivorship, if one party dies the other receives full title to the property.

Two or more persons may own property as <u>joint tenants with the right of survivorship.</u> This means that if one party dies the other receives full title to the property.

Another common form of property ownership is a <u>tenancy by the entirety.</u> This is a legal form of ownership which applies to property jointly owned by married couples with the right of survivorship.

In either a joint tenancy or a tenancy by the entirety, the entire interest in the property passes to the surviving owner. Thus, the law dictates that property held in a joint tenancy or in a tenancy by the entirety passes outside a will.

CASE IN POINT

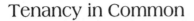

Tenancy in Common

Jack and his neighbor Bob decide to purchase a small lakeside lot for the purpose of having a spot where they can fish together each weekend. They purchase the lot as <u>tenants in common.</u> Jack contributes 60 percent of the purchase price, and Bob contributes the remaining 40 percent. As tenants in common, either Jack or Bob may sell or give his interest in the lot to a third party. Several years later, Jack sells his 60 percent interest in the lot to Bill. Bob dies, leaving his 40 percent interest in the lot to Susan. Now Bill and Susan own the lot as tenants in common. Bill is the owner of 60 percent of the interest in the lot, and Susan holds a 40 percent ownership interest in the lot. If the property is sold, Bill will receive 60 percent of the proceeds of the sale and Susan will receive the remaining 40 percent.

Joint Tenancy with the Right of Survivorship

Barbara and Jean purchase a townhouse from Ethel as <u>joint tenants with the right of survivorship.</u> Both Barbara and Jean own an undivided interest in the townhouse, meaning that each has an equal right to possess the entire property. Upon Jean's death, Barbara automatically owns 100 percent of the property since she survived Jean. This result follows "by operation of law" regardless of any contrary provisions in Jean's will. While they are living, either Barbara or Jean may sell her interest to a third party.

If Jean sells her interest to Wanda, the joint tenancy is automatically converted to a <u>tenancy in common,</u> so Wanda and Barbara will own the townhouse as tenants in common.

Tenancy by the Entirety

<u>Tenancy by the entirety</u> is similar to a joint tenancy in that there is a right of survivorship. However, only a husband and wife can own property as tenants by the entirety. If Steve and Tracy as husband and wife own a house as tenants by the entirety, neither can convey his or her interest to a third party without the consent of the other. In addition, the creditors of one spouse may not use tenancy by the entirety property to satisfy any outstanding judgments against one individual spouse.

Convenience Accounts with a Survivorship Right

If anything other than a survivorship account is intended, this should be clearly specified in writing.

Two or more persons may establish a bank account as joint tenants with the right of survivorship merely for convenience. Typically, one joint tenant will deposit all funds in the joint account and add the name of a second person. The second person's name is added to ensure ready access to the funds in the account in the event the person opening the account dies or becomes incapacitated. In the event of such an arrangement, a question may arise regarding the true intent of the person who opened the account. Did he really intend to create a survivorship account or did he merely do it as a matter of convenience? If anything other than a survivorship account is intended, this should be clearly specified in writing.

CASE IN POINT

Cindy Cochrane was the beneficiary of an insurance policy on the life of her husband Carl. When Carl died, the proceeds of this policy, $100,000, were paid to Cindy. Cindy deposited all of these funds in a joint bank account in her name and in the name of her daughter, Mimi, as joint tenants with a right of survivorship. Cindy told Mimi that if she became disabled or died, Mimi would have access to these funds to pay any necessary expenses. Cindy advised Mimi that when she (Cindy) died, these funds should be divided equally between Mimi and her two sisters.

It appears that Cindy did not intend for Mimi to become the sole owner of the account at Cindy's death. But following Cindy's death, Mimi may assert that she is the sole owner of the property by operation of law. It would then be necessary for Mimi's sisters to file an action in court and attempt to prove that Cindy's true intent was that all three sisters would share any funds remaining in the account at Cindy's death.

In many states the arrangement between Cindy and Mimi would not be treated as a true joint tenancy, but merely as a <u>convenience account.</u> In such a situation, it would be preferable for Cindy to clearly specify in writing exactly how she wanted the proceeds of the account distributed at her death.

If Cindy fails to do so, it would be necessary for a court to determine Cindy's true intent in establishing the account. Regardless of the outcome of the action, the relationship of Cindy's daughters may be irreparably damaged and all parties may incur considerable legal expenses.

Community Property

Special laws may affect individuals who reside in one of the nine community property states. These states are Arizona, California, Idaho, Louisiana, Nevada, New Mexico, Texas, Washington and Wisconsin. In a community property state each spouse shares equally in all property acquired during the marriage. Each spouse is deemed to own one-half of all property earned during the marriage regardless of whether one spouse actually earned more money than the other.

In a community property state each spouse shares equally in all property acquired during the marriage.

In each community property state all property is divided into one of two categories: separate property and community property. Separate property includes all property owned at the time of the marriage or acquired during the marriage by gift or inheritance. Separate property belongs to only one spouse and is not subject to any claims of the other spouse.

All property that is not separate property is community property, the presumption being that all other property acquired during the marriage is community property and is subject to the claims of the other spouse. This presumption may be refuted only by convincing evidence.

CASE IN POINT

Community Property

Roberta and Gene are a married couple who live in California. Roberta is an attorney who earns $100,000 per year. Gene works as the managing director of a theater and earns $50,000 per year. Each year Roberta places $10,000 from her salary in a savings account at the Bank of Southern California. In her will she specifies that the savings account should be left to her sister Tricia. On the date of Roberta's death the savings account contains $40,000.

Since the funds in the account were derived from funds Roberta earned while married to Gene, the money is community property. Under the terms of Roberta's will, only one-half of the account ($20,000) will pass to Tricia because Gene has a community property interest in the other half of the account. Thus, Gene will also receive $20,000.

Separate Property

Suppose all of the facts in the above example are the same except that the source of the funds in the savings account is an inheritance from Roberta's mother. In that case Tricia would receive the entire $40,000 because Roberta received the money in the savings account as a bequest in a will. It is Roberta's separate property. As such, Gene has no claim to the funds and Roberta is free to distribute them in accordance with her wishes.

Restrictions on Ability to Transfer Property

A person's ability to transfer property may be subject to other restrictions. Two common restrictions apply to persons who own a life estate or a future interest in property.

CASE IN POINT

Life Estate

Laura, a wealthy widow, has two adult children, Meg and Reid. Meg is married and has three children of her own. Reid has never married and has always lived with his mother in Laura's large house. In her will Laura specifies that Reid will have "a life estate" in her house, and that upon his death Meg will become the owner of the house.

When Laura dies, Reid will have the right to remain in the house until he dies. He is responsible for all expenses incurred in maintaining the property, such as taxes and utilities. When Reid dies, however, the property transfers to Meg under the terms of Laura's will. Any provision in Reid's will regarding the property is void because Reid's rights to the property terminate upon his death. Once the property is transferred to Meg, she owns the property outright, or in legal terms, <u>in fee simple absolute,</u> meaning ownership without restrictions. Meg may keep the property or she may sell it. She is free to transfer the property in her will.

Future Interest

Suppose in the above example Laura's will specifies that upon her death her son Reid would have the right to use the house for three years. At the expiration of the three-year period, Meg would become the owner of the house in fee simple absolute, if she survives Reid.

In this scenario, when Laura dies, Reid has exclusive rights to use and live in Laura's house for three years. At the end of the three-year period, however, Reid's rights to use the house terminate and the house will transfer to Meg. At Laura's death it is impossible to determine whether Meg will be living at the end of the three-year period. Her interest in the house is an "uncertain" or "indefinite" future interest. If Meg is still living at the end of the three year period, however, she will own the house in fee simple absolute.

Asset Analysis

The first step in developing any estate plan is to identify the assets one has and the restrictions, if any, on one's ability to transfer these assets. If property passes either by contract or by operation of law, it will not be affected by the terms of a will or trust. If necessary, individuals should restructure ownership of their holdings to ensure that their estate planning goals are met.

Restructuring ownership of holdings may be necessary to ensure that estate planning goals are met.

The checklist reproduced at the end of this chapter should serve as a helpful starting point in evaluating the nature and extent of one's assets. When this process is completed, the estate planning process in ready to begin.

Asset and Estate Concerns Checklist

Family Members	Name	Age	Marital Status	Occupation
Testator:				
Spouse:				
Children:				
Grandchildren:				
Others: (Dependents)				
(Relatives)				

Domicile of Testator	Address	Phone No.	City	County	State
Home:					
Other places of residence: (homes, cottages, etc.)					
Prior residences over past 10 years, if any:					

BUSINESS

Name of Business: _____

Business Address: _____

Phone Number: _____

Type of Business (purpose): _____

Form of Ownership: _____

Sole Proprietor: _____

Partner: _____

Corporation: _____

Other: _____

FAMILY MATTERS

Previous marriages: _____

_____

Children of previous marriage: _____

_____

Settlement information: _____

_____

Special dependency cases: _____

_____

Handicapped (child, parent, relative: _____

_____

TRUSTS

Spendthrift child: _____

_____

Life estate to be transferred: _____

Persons to be disinherited (specific reasons listed below): _____

_____

_____

_____

_____

Advancements (property previously transferred before testator's death:

_____

_____

_____

_____

_____

_____

FAMILY ADVISERS

	Name	Address	Telephone No.

Accountant: _____

Attorney: _____

Banker: _____

_____

Clergyman: _____

Doctor: _____

Insurance Agent: _____

Others: _____

_____

CASH   Value   Location

Cash and Checking Accounts: _____

_____

Savings Accounts: _____

_____

STOCKS AND BONDS

Stocks (Name and no. of shares): _____

_____

Stock options: _____

U.S. Govt. Bonds: _____

Municipal Bonds: _____

Other: _____

_____

_____

_____

PERSONAL PROPERTY

Item	Value	Location

Furniture and Household Goods: _____

_____

Furs and Jewelry: _____

_____

Automobiles (type and year): _____

(1) _____

(2) _____

Clothing and Personal Effects: _____

_____

Other: _____

REAL PROPERTY

Residential: _____

_____

Business Building: _____

Recreational (summer cottage: _____

Other: _____

_____

RECEIVABLES

Promissory notes (payable to client): _____

_____

Contract for deed (client is seller): _____

_____

Other: _____

_____

EMPLOYEE, CORPORATE AND OTHER BENEFITS

Item	Value	Location
Pension Plan:		
Stock Bonus:		
Profit-sharing Plan:		
Health Insurance - Accident & Health:		
Medical & Surgical:		
Hospitalization:		
Social Security:		
Veterans Benefits:		

INTERESTS IN TRUSTS OR OTHER ESTATES

LIFE INSURANCE AND ANNUITIES DATA

Insurance Agent:_____Phone: _____

Name/Policy No: _____

Location of Policy: _____

Annual Premium: _____

Cash Value: _____

Loan on Cash Value of Policy: _____

Face or Death Value: _____

Straight Life or Term: _____

Endowment or Annuity: _____

Group Life Insurance: _____

Miscellaneous Property: _____

TOTAL ASSEST (value): _____

LIABILITIES

Item	Value	Location

Promissory Notes
(to banks, loan companies,
individuals, etc): _____

_____

Mortgages on Real Property: _____

_____

Payments on Contracts
for Deeds: _____

_____

Charge Accounts and
Installment Purchases: _____

_____

Loans on Insurance Policies: _____

Business debts: _____

Enforceable Pledges to
Charitable and Religious
Organizations: _____

_____

Taxes Owed: _____

TOTAL LIABILITIES: _____

_____

ASSET LOCATION; PERSONAL STATISTICS

Social Security No.: _____

Birth Certificate: _____

Deeds - Real Estate: _____

Contracts for Deed: _____

Leases: _____

Partnership Agreements: _____

Corporation Documents: _____

Charter Bylaws: _____

Corporation Stock: _____

Certificates: _____

Options: _____

Bonds and other Debentures: _____

Divorce Decree: _____

Antenuptial Agreements: _____

Trusts: _____

Documents Granting Powers of Appointment: _____

_____

Life Insurance Policies: _____

Other Insurance Policies: _____

Income and Gift Tax Returns (last 3 years): _____

_____

Federal: _____

State: _____

Current Will: _____

CHAPTER 2

Preparing
A Will

Preparing a Will

A will properly prepared ensures that a person's estate is distributed to the intended beneficiaries.

The preparation of an estate plan generally involves the preparation of a <u>will.</u> A will is a written legal document that instructs how an individual's property should be distributed after death. A carefully drafted will can usually be prepared by an experienced attorney at a relatively modest cost. If properly prepared, it ensures that a person's estate is distributed to the intended beneficiaries in an orderly manner as soon as possible after death.

Drafting a Valid Will

The technical requirements for a valid will vary from state to state. In general, any person of sound mind and who is 18 years of age or older can make a will.[2] Most states require that the will be in writing and signed by the <u>testator</u> (the person writing the will) in the presence of two or more disinterested witnesses.

A disinterested witness is an individual who is not entitled to receive a portion of the testator's estate, either through the will or pursuant to state law if the testator dies without a valid will. In some states, a will need not be witnessed if it is written entirely in the handwriting of the testator. A will written entirely in the handwriting of the testator is known as a <u>holographic will.</u>

A valid will may be amended by creating a new will or by revoking an old will. The requirements for validly revoking an existing will vary from state to state, but revocation is usually achieved by physically destroying an old will or by executing a new will that clearly expresses the testator's intent to revoke all former wills.

Why Have a Will?

The most important reason for preparing a will is that it permits an individual to determine how his property will be distributed after death. Wills may also help in minimizing estate taxes or establishing guardian provisions for minor children.

[2] Individuals must be 19 years of age or older to execute a will in Wyoming.

When a person dies, he is referred to as the "decedent." If a person dies with a valid will, he has died "testate." In contrast, if he dies without a will, he has died "intestate."

If a person dies intestate, his assets will be distributed in accordance with state law without regard to his wishes. Each state has its own laws for determining which survivors will inherit the assets of a person who dies without a valid will. These laws are referred to as the laws of intestate succession.

If a person dies without a will, his assets will be distributed in accordance with state law without regard to his wishes.

Most state laws provide that an individual's property will be distributed among members of his immediate family, but the amount of property passing to a specific individual varies from state to state. In certain states, if a married person dies intestate and is survived by a spouse and children, his property will be divided between his spouse and his children. In other states, however, a share of an individual's property may be divided among a surviving spouse, children, parents or even brothers and sisters. Since the laws of intestate succession vary from state to state, it is impossible to state a general rule. The laws of intestate succession only apply if an individual dies without having executed a valid will.

In most cases, state law also determines the percentage of assets each recipient may receive. These formulas of distribution vary from state to state. For example, under the laws of intestate succession in some states, a surviving spouse may inherit all of the decedent's real and personal property if there are no surviving children. If there are surviving children or other descendants of the deceased spouse, such as surviving parents, brothers or sisters, the surviving spouse may receive as little as one-third of the real and personal property and the remainder may be divided among the other survivors. This may happen even though the surviving spouse needs the assets and the parents, brothers and sisters have been out of touch for years. Therefore, if an individual wants to ensure that his property is distributed in accordance with his wishes, it is essential that he execute a valid will.

CASE IN POINT

Jane Jones, the widow of John Jones, owns a home in Maryland worth approximately $200,000. The mortgage on this home is fully paid off. Jane's other assets include bank accounts, stocks and bonds, and proceeds from an insurance policy of her deceased husband. The total value of these assets is $400,000. These are her only assets other than such personal effects as clothing, household furniture and an automobile. Jane receives a monthly survivor annuity in an amount sufficient to satisfy all of her needs.

Jane has three adult children, Peter, Sam and Mary. Peter and Mary are self-supporting, but Sam is handicapped. While he receives a small Social Security benefit, he lives with his mother and depends on her for support and to manage his affairs. Jane is concerned about what will happen to Sam when she dies.

She wants Sam to remain in the family home and she wants most of her assets to be used to support him. Jane has no will.

If Jane dies without a will, an interested party must petition the court and ask to be appointed administrator. Her property will be divided into three equal shares with one share going to each child. Unless the court finds that Sam is incompetent to manage his affairs, he will be paid his one-third share. His brother, sister or other interested party will be required to petition the court to be appointed as Sam's guardian. A properly prepared will could help avoid this result and properly provide for Sam's care and guardianship.

Property Passing Outside of the Will

The essential element in preparing a will is to determine the form in which any property is owned.

The discussion in Chapter 1 illustrates that not all of a decedent's property passes under a will. If property passes by an insurance contract or through a joint tenancy or tenancy by the entirety, it will not be affected by the terms of a will. Thus, an essential element in preparing a will is to determine the form in which any property is owned. If necessary, individuals should restructure ownership of their holdings to ensure that estate planning goals are met.

CASE IN POINT

Jeff and Mary Jones are husband and wife and they own their home in Virginia as tenants by the entirety. They have four self-supporting children. Jeff has other assets in his name worth approximately $300,000. Jeff also purchases a life insurance policy with a face value of $100,000 and names Mary beneficiary of the policy. Although he would like all of these assets to go to Mary upon his death, Jeff dies before he ever writes a will. Under Virginia law, his interest in the family home will pass to Mary by operation of law because she is the surviving tenant.

Mary will also receive the life insurance proceeds because she is named beneficiary in this policy and the insurance company has a contractual obligation to pay the proceeds to her. Since Jeff never wrote a will, the Virginia laws of intestate succession will dictate how the remainder of his property is to be distributed.

Revisions to a Will

Once a will has been drafted and signed, it cannot merely be stored in a safe deposit box and ignored. Life is full of changes and a will must be revised to reflect these changes. Peculiar rules may affect a person who fails to keep his will up-to-date. In some states, for example, a will may be revoked by marriage unless it expressly states that it was prepared in contemplation of a particular marriage and shall not be revoked by that marriage. Divorce can either revoke an entire will or only those provisions which favor the former spouse. Similarly, in some states a legally separated spouse may inherit from the decedent's estate if the decedent does not revise his will, or dies without a will, before a final decree of divorce is entered. All of this depends on state law. Thus, if an individual's marital status changes, it may be prudent to revise a will.

Life is full of changes and a will must be revised to reflect these changes.

CASE IN POINT

Harry, a wealthy bachelor, drafts a will in which he leaves his entire estate to his devoted spinster sister, Toni. Two years later, Harry marries Norma. He does not revise his will. Harry is unexpectedly killed when he sustains an injury while skiing on vacation. Toni asserts that Harry's entire estate should pass to her. In many states, however, Norma immediately acquires certain rights by operation of law once she becomes Harry's wife. Since she was not mentioned in his will, his entire will could be declared invalid, meaning that Toni will receive nothing and Norma may receive his entire estate under the laws of intestate succession. (See page 35 for a discussion of Norma's right to a spousal share of Harry's estate.) In other states, Norma may be permitted to receive her intestate share of Harry's estate, and the balance of Harry's property will pass to Toni under Harry's will.

Birth or Adoption of Children

The birth or adoption of children may also change the estate planning scheme. Some states have enacted statutes that prohibit children or grandchildren born after a will is executed from receiving a share of the testator's property unless the testator specifies his desire to provide for after-born children in his will. In contrast, other states specifically provide a share of the estate to a child born after a will was drafted. In some cases, the testator may intentionally attempt to exclude his spouse or children from receiving a share of his estate, yet some state laws may defeat such intent and create a gift to the excluded relatives against the testator's wishes.

CASE IN POINT

Many states provide protection to children who are born after a testator drafts a will. Shirley drafts a will after her daughter Liza is born leaving one-half of her property to her husband, Brian, and the remaining one-half to Liza. Two years later, Shirley dies from complications encountered during the birth of her son, Richard.

In many states, the law would provide her new son Richard with the right to receive his intestate share of his mother's estate because he was not mentioned in her will. Thus, it is unclear whether she intended to provide for him. If Shirley had revised her will after Richard was born, and indicated that she still wished to leave all of her property to Liza and nothing to Richard, Richard would probably have no claim against Shirley's estate. Most states permit an individual to leave property to persons other than their children. Children are usually provided protection in cases where they are born after the testator has executed a will that is silent on the issue of how property to after-born children should be treated.

A Codicil

Once a will is prepared, it may be amended or revoked at any time before the maker's death, as long as the maker is competent. A person is competent if he is 18 years of age (19 in Wyoming) or older and is capable of understanding the effects of his actions. A simple amendment to a will is called a codicil and may be necessary if circumstances change any of the situations addressed in the will.

Spousal Share

In most states, a surviving spouse is entitled to a specified share of the decedent's assets.

Virtually every state has laws that prohibit an individual from disinheriting a surviving spouse. In most states, a surviving spouse is entitled to a specified share of the decedent's assets (frequently one-half or one-third.) This is known as the spouse's statutory share. A surviving spouse who is unhappy with the provisions of the decedent's will may sometimes choose not to accept the amount given to him or her in the will and receive instead the amount provided by law, known as the statutory share. For example, a wealthy woman may wish to disinherit her husband. As such, she may provide in her will that she leaves her husband "the sum of one (1) dollar." At the time of her death, the widow lived in a state whose laws provide the husband an automatic right to one-third of her property. The husband might argue successfully that at a minimum he is entitled to receive his one-third share. Accordingly, he may "renounce" the wife's will and take his one-third statutory share of her estate. The remaining two-thirds of the wife's estate would be distributed in accordance with the instructions in the wife's will.

The wife may be able to avoid this result by reducing the assets which she owns at her death either through lifetime gifts to other beneficiaries, by creating joint ownership of assets with the right of survivorship with third persons, or by creating a trust. What is important to understand is that these problems can be minimized with careful estate planning.

Executor, Personal Representative or Administrator

The executor of a will takes the steps necessary to implement the wishes of the decedent.

An individual must be appointed to ensure that a decedent's wishes as expressed in the will are carried out. This person is known as the <u>executor</u> (or <u>executrix,</u> if female) or personal representative. The terms executor or personal representative are used interchangeably. The person appointed to this position takes the steps necessary to implement the wishes of the decedent. He or she pays all bills, collects all debts and distributes all property of the decedent. When this process is completed, the executor or personal representative closes the estate.

If an individual dies without a valid will, it is also necessary for an individual to take charge of the decedent's affairs. If there is no will, an interested party (usually a close friend or relative) must ask the court to appoint a personal representative. In this situation, the personal representative is generally known as an <u>administrator</u> (or <u>administratrix,</u> if female.) The functions of a personal representative, executor or administrator are identical, namely, to act on the decedent's behalf to wind up his affairs.

Guardians

A will also affords an individual the opportunity to select a <u>guardian</u> to care for minor children or other persons who may not be competent to manage their affairs. If a guardian is not named, and both parents of minor children die or become incapacitated, the state court will name an adult to serve as guardian of the minor. Although the procedures vary from state to state, most courts strive to appoint an individual who is a relative and otherwise fit to supervise the minor. When drafting a will or trust, a professional advisor can ensure that the persons preparing the will appoint the guardian they wish.

There may be restrictions which limit certain individuals from serving as executors or guardians, such as foreign citizenship or out-of-state residency.

CASE IN POINT

John and Jennifer live in New York and have two minor children, Sarah and Sue. Jennifer's only living relative is a cousin, Jim, who lives in New Jersey. John has one sister, Ann, who lives in Canada. Under the laws of certain states, Ann would be appointed guardian of Sara and Sue if John and Jennifer die or become incapacitated without having named a guardian. John and Jennifer do not want Sarah and Sue to be reared in Canada, so they execute a document naming Jim the guardian of their children. This document, in all likelihood, would be honored if John and Jennifer both die or become incapacitated even though as their aunt, Ann is more closely related by blood to Sarah and Sue than Jim, who is a distant cousin of the children.

Further Considerations

A carefully drawn will may reduce the expense of administering an estate by giving the executor the authority to act without unnecessary delay. For example, many states require an executor to obtain permission from the probate court to complete certain tasks such as the sale of the decedent's real property. The probate court is a division of the state court designed to handle all matters concerning wills and estate administration.

A properly drafted will may minimize the role of the probate court in the administration of the estate.

If a will is properly drafted, it may minimize the role of the probate court in the administration of the estate, reducing the expense of the probate process, expediting the settlement of the estate, and hastening the disposition of assets to the named beneficiaries.

Summary

In general a will must be written and witnessed in a manner provided by law. The first and last pages of a typical will appear at the end of this chapter. The law does not require that valid wills be drafted by an attorney. The complexities of estate planning involved in the preparation of wills may, however, make it prudent to seek the benefit of a lawyer's expertise.

(FIRST AND LAST PAGES OF SIMPLE WILL)

LAST WILL AND TESTAMENT
OF
MICHAEL A. SMITH

I, Michael A. Smith, residing and domiciled in Washington, D.C., being over the age of eighteen (18) years, declare this writing my Last Will and Testament and revoke all other wills, codicils and testamentary dispositions made by me before this date.

ARTICLE I

At the date of execution of the Will, I am married to SAMANTHA B. SMITH, described throughout this Will as "my wife," and we have two children, LOLA SMITH of Washington, D.C., and TIFFANY EPPERLY of Roanoke, Virginia.

ARTICLE II

A. I direct my Executor to pay any judicially enforceable debts I may have at the time of my death; the expenses of my last illness; the expenses of a funeral or memorial service appropriate to my station in life and custom of living without court order and without regard to any statutory limitation thereto; and any unpaid charitable pledges evidenced by a writing signed by me, whether or not these are judicially enforceable obligations.

If there is a complete failure of takers under the preceding Articles of the Will, I give, bequeath and devise one-half of the rest and residue of my estate to my heirs and one-half of the rest and residue of my estate to the heirs of my wife as determined at the time of my death, pursuant to Sections 19-301 through 19-321 of the Code of the District of Columbia as it is written on the date of this Will.

IN WITNESS WHEREOF, I have hereunto set my hand and seal to this, my Last Will and Testament, and I have affixed my initials for better identification on the bottom of this and _____preceding pages, this _____day of _____, 1994.

_____
MICHAEL A. SMITH

The foregoing will, consisting of _____ type-written pages, numbered one through _____ was signed, published and declared by the Testator, MICHAEL A. SMITH, to be his Last Will and Testament, in the presence of us, all present at the same time, who at his request, in his presence and in the presence of each other, have hereunto subscribed our names as witnesses this _____day of _____, 1994.

NAME   ADDRESS

Printed_____Street_____

Signature_____City_____

Printed_____Street_____

Signature_____City_____

Printed_____Street_____

Signature_____City_____

CITY OF WASHINGTON
DISTRICT OF COLUMBIA

Before me, the undersigned authority, in this day, personally appeared MICHAEL A. SMITH, _____, _____, and _____, known to me to be the Testator and the witnesses, respectively, whose names are signed to the attached and foregoing instrument and all of these persons being by me first duly sworn, MICHAEL A. SMITH, the Testator, declared to me and to the witnesses in my presence, that said instrument is his Last Will and Testament and that he had willingly signed and executed it in the presence of said witnesses as his free and voluntary act for the purposes therein expressed; that said witnesses stated before me that the foregoing Will was executed and acknowledged by the Testator as his Last Will and Testament in the presence of said witnesses who, in the presence of Testator and at his request, and the presence of each other, did subscribe their names thereto as attesting witnesses on the day of the date of said Will, and that the Testator at the time of execution of said Will was over the age of eighteen (18) years and of sound and disposing mind and memory.

_____
MICHAEL A. SMITH

WITNESSES:

_____

_____

_____

Subscribed, sworn and acknowledged before my by MICHAEL A. SMITH, the Testator; subscribed and sworn before me by _____, _____, and _____, witnesses, this _____ day of _____, 1994.

_____
NOTARY PUBLIC

My commission expires:

CHAPTER 3

Living Wills And Durable Powers of Attorney

Living Wills and Durable Powers of Attorney

Doctors tell a patient's family that the patient lying in a hospital bed in a coma has no realistic possibility of regaining consciousness. With continued medical support, the patient may linger indefinitely, but if the medical support is withdrawn, the patient will probably die within a matter of hours.

On countless occasions the patient expressed a desire not to have life sustained artificially. The family asks hospital personnel to discontinue life-sustaining treatment, but the hospital refuses, noting that the hospital may be liable if it takes such a measure without the patient's consent.

The patient, who cannot give the required consent because he is incompetent, remains in a coma and dies eight years later, leaving survivors emotionally and financially drained.

The right of a terminally ill individual's family to have life support systems removed was the subject of a much publicized U.S. Supreme Court case, *Cruzan v. Missouri Department of Health,* in June of 1990. The court ruled that a hospital could not take the extraordinary measure of withdrawing life sustaining medical treatment without obtaining written authority from the patient while she was competent. Thus, the scenario described above could be replayed unless an individual executes legal documents allowing the removal of artificial life support systems.

The *Cruzan* case involved a young woman named Nancy Cruzan who was left in a permanent vegetative state following an automobile accident. Prior to the accident, she had stated that she never wanted her life artificially sustained by medical treatment if there was no hope of her recovery, but she had never reduced her wishes to writing. Fearing liability, the hospital refused to remove a food and hydration tube that kept Ms. Cruzan alive, despite her parents' request that the tube be removed. The Supreme Court agreed with the hospital, even though experts estimate that Ms. Cruzan could linger another 30 years. The court also recognized that it is possible to avoid the painful consequences described in *Cruzan* by following the legally approved methods specified in various state laws.

Many states have enacted legislation allowing individuals to draft a <u>living will,</u> a <u>durable power of attorney,</u> a <u>health care power of attorney,</u> or all three. By using these tools, a competent individual may control fundamental medical decisions that may affect his body in the future. In the District of Columbia, for example, anyone who is 18 years of age or older may execute a document that directs the withholding or withdrawal of life-sustaining procedures in the event of a terminal illness. If properly drafted, the document should remain valid, even if the individual is subsequently rendered unconscious or otherwise mentally incompetent.

Powers of Attorney

Through a durable power of attorney, a person, while competent, designates a trusted friend or relative (designated as the "attorney-in-fact") to make major financial decisions for the person should he become disabled in the future.

Similarly, through a health care power of attorney, a person designates another to make health care decisions for him in the event of incompetency.

The individual designated "attorney-in-fact" can evaluate changing financial circumstances or information provided by medical personnel and determine which courses of action will be in the patient's best interest and most likely consistent with the patient's wishes.

Since medical technology and circumstances change from the date a person executes a power of attorney to the date that a person may become incapacitated, a durable power of attorney or a health care power of attorney offer both flexibility and protection of the individual's best interests.

A durable power of attorney or a health care power of attorney offer flexibility and protection of the individual's best interest.

Although it is possible to grant health care and financial decision-making power for the same attorney-in-fact in one document, there are many disadvantages to combining these objectives in one document. For example, if the documents are ever needed, both the financial institutions and the health care provider will wish to retain an original document in their files.

Since many persons consider the health care provisions to be highly personal and sensitive, they may feel uncomfortable with the knowledge that this highly private matter will be disclosed to financial officers who have no need for this information.

The American Bar Association has provided the authors of this book with a list of states which recognize health care powers of attorney and living wills (see page 46). Each state that recognizes either health care powers or attorney and/or living wills has been marked with an X. If you do not find your state listed, contact the state Agency on Aging in your area or your local Bar Association for further information.

A Living Will

A living will may be the better document for those who oppose the use of life-support systems.

A living will, in contrast, may be less flexible. Since living wills frequently specify that no life-support systems may be utilized under any circumstances, a living will may limit the discretion of individuals attending the patient and leave no room for medical advancements. For persons who strongly oppose the use of life-support systems under any circumstances, however, a living will may be the better document.

Implementation of the Documents

To ensure that the patient's wishes are honored, it is essential that persons involved in making any decision to terminate life support systems are aware of their appointment. The person designated as attorney-in-fact or executor should be notified of the appointment and should agree to it. The designee should also be given a copy of the appointment document. In addition, it may be advisable to give the patient's health care provider a copy of the durable power of attorney or living will. The document should be kept by the hospital with the patient's medical chart once health care is required so that the physicians will have ready access to it in the event a quick decision is necessary.

Both a durable power of attorney and a living will must be carefully drafted to ensure that they conform with the legal formalities set forth in applicable state laws, particularly since the laws for drafting these documents are highly technical.

The District of Columbia law, for example, requires that either a durable power of attorney or a living will must be signed in the presence of two witnesses, neither of whom may be a close relative, an employee of the patient's health care facility, or an attending physician of the individual who is drafting the document. Many states also require the witnesses to sign an affidavit saying that they are not related to the individual and will not receive all or a portion of his property when he dies.

Since questions may arise about the competency of an individual to draft a durable power of attorney or a living will if the individual is already suffering from debilitating disabilities, a growing number of people are drafting such documents while they enjoy good physical and mental health.

Estate planners, accountants, retirement organizations, and such facilities as nursing homes, hospices and hospitals are increasingly able to provide assistance to those with questions about these legal documents.

Both a durable power of attorney and a living will must be carefully drafted.

STATE	HEALTH CARE POA*	LIVING WILL	STATE	HEALTH CARE POA*	LIVING WILL
Alabama		X	Missouri	X	X
Arkansas	X	X	Montana	X	X
Arizona	X	X	Nevada	X	X
Alaska	X	X	New Hampshire	X	X
California	X	X	New Mexico	X	X
Colorado	X	X	New York	X	
Connecticut	X	X	North Carolina	X	X
Delaware	X	X	North Dakota	X	X
District of Columbia	X	X	Ohio	X	X
Florida	X	X	Oklahoma	X	X
Georgia	X	X	Oregon	X	X
Hawaii	X	X	Pennsylvania	X	X
Idaho	X	X	Rhode Island	X	X
Illinois	X	X	South Carolina	X	X
Indiana	X	X	South Dakota	X	X
Iowa	X	X	Tennessee	X	X
Kansas	X	X	Texas	X	X
Kentucky	X	X	Utah	X	X
Lousiana	X	X	Vermont	X	X
Maine	X	X	Virginia	X	X
Maryland	X	X	Washington	X	X
Massachusetts	X		West Virginia	X	X
Michigan	X		Wisconsin	X	X
Minnesota	X	X	Wyoming	X	X
Mississippi	X	X			

*POA = Power of Attorney

CHAPTER 4

Using Will and Trust Kits for Estate Planning

Using Will and Trust Kits for Estate Planning

While many people acknowledge the need for estate planning, it is one of life's "duties" that is often postponed. Even many accomplished lawyers are guilty of not writing their wills. Why is this so, when both the financial and emotional stakes are often so high?

People do not like facing their own mortality and often postpone the duty of estate planning.

First, people do not like facing their own mortality. They assume that if there is no will, death is not imminent.

Second, estate planning requires a great deal of thought. Should the heirloom jewelry go to Katy or Joan? Should Sam, a spendthrift, get an equal share of the money? What should be done about an incompetent child who needs special treatment? If nothing is left to the child, will the state pick up the child's care through welfare and Medicaid programs? Do the parents have an obligation to continue support, if they can, after they themselves die?

Third, many individuals think their assets are insufficient to require estate planning. At today's prices, however, almost anyone who owns a house, car, and furniture may benefit from estate planning.

Fourth, many people do not want to pay lawyers for the time it takes to perform quality estate planning. Because estate laws and tax laws are complicated and because lawyer's fees are high, estate planning can be expensive. The fees charged by an attorney naturally vary from community to community and from law firm to law firm within a given community. A simple will may cost as little as $75 or as much as $500. Typical attorneys' fees for drafting a trust range from $800 to $2,500 depending upon the complexity of an individual's situation.

While trusts are usually more expensive, their benefits may result in substantial future savings.

Many individuals may be startled to discover that although will and trust kits are believed to be inexpensive alternatives to obtaining a professional document prepared by an attorney, their costs may range from $25 for a simple will kit to several thousand dollars for the complex instructions and forms needed to draft a trust. If there are sizable assets or personal complications, the money invested in estate planning will often be returned many times over when one dies. The savings, of course, will be to the heirs, not the decedent, and some people simply adopt the attitude, "Let them worry about it when they get it."

The more responsible attitude, however, recognizes the value of an estate and works to maximize its worth and minimize the headaches it will place on survivors.

Advantages of Using a Kit

One way in which more individuals are recognizing their responsibilities but simplifying the process and minimizing costs is by utilizing commercial "will" or "trust" kits. While such kits are rather simple, straightforward, and general, it is certainly better to use a kit than to die with no will or trust at all. Many persons using these kits do so because they consider them less expensive than hiring a lawyer to prepare a will.

It is certainly better to use a kit than to die with no will or trust at all.

At the very least, a written document reflects a person's wishes with respect to the disposition of property. If the will is challenged by survivors and found to be invalid, courts may not be bound by such wishes.

In some instances, however, will and trust kits may provide the same result a person would achieve if he paid hundreds of dollars to a professional estate planner. This is particularly true if the estate is moderate and its disposition is to immediate family.

A good kit may also serve as an excellent educational aid. It may allow persons to familiarize themselves with the will, trust, and probate process so they can more effectively discuss their concerns with a professional. Most kits acknowledge that they are not necessarily for everyone and that they are not a substitute for the advice of a competent professional.

In some cases, though, the use of a kit may prove to be "penny-wise and pound-foolish." A person may be left with a will or trust which is worth little more than the small price he paid for the kit.

Persons who have substantial assets or wish to leave property to persons or organizations other than their immediate family almost always need professional, individually-tailored advice. The key question, then, is determining who should use a kit and who should not.

Advantages of Professional Advice

When people die, survivors must initially cope with the emotional reaction of their loss, but as the mourning period progresses, survivors must cope with the often complicated and difficult task of managing the financial affairs of the deceased.

Poor planning, or no planning can result in disagreements among survivors and mismanagement of the decedent's assets.

Careful estate planning helps ensure that this inevitable task is completed as efficiently and painlessly as possible.

Poor planning, or no planning, on the other hand, can result in disagreements among survivors and result in mismanagement of the decedent's assets by loved ones incapable of handling complicated financial affairs.

Attorneys generally spend several hours helping clients determine whether a simple will or trust can accomplish the person's objectives. Among key questions are:

• How should the property be disposed of?

• Which relatives, friends, or charities are to be named as recipients of the property?

• Are there children for whom a guardian should be named or a trust established?

• Are there minor or adult children who have special medical, educational, or support needs?

- Is it possible that there will be adopted children or children born after the will is executed?

- What should be done if the named individual does not survive the testator or otherwise refuses the gift?

While these questions may seem wide-ranging and inapplicable to the client, an attorney seeks to provide for every possible contingency in a client's will or trust and to structure the will or trust so the client need not revise it each time he experiences minor changes in circumstances.

Attorneys also counsel clients on the tax implications of their decisions. While estate planning should not be based solely on tax considerations, a thorough understanding of how taxes impact an estate can save and protect assets for the benefit of heirs.

For example, a frequent misconception is that probate can always be avoided by establishing trusts as substitutes for wills. In some states, though, surviving spouses and children have rights to a minimal share of a deceased person's estate and may be able to petition the court for a portion of the deceased's property, even if the deceased made other arrangements in a trust to leave his property to a third party.

A carefully planned estate may assure that there is no probate, or is limited in scope.

A carefully planned estate may assure that there is no probate, or if there is, that it is imited in scope. Moreover, proper planning may eliminate the possibility of a successful challenge to a testator's wishes by (1) designating to a surviving spouse or children (in the will or in another instrument) at least the minimum legally required portion of the estate; and (2) drafting a pour-over will. A pour-over will designates the trust as recipient of all of the property owned on the date of death which has not been otherwise disposed. The simple pour-over will is then filed with the probate court where the estate is opened, all outstanding creditors and taxes are paid, and the estate is closed.

These are the sort of complicated legalities for which one pays an attorney.

The Problems with Kits

Estate planning often must be tailored for each client. Kits, however, are usually general. For example, a father may draft a will using a kit that designates "my house located at 1211 Main St., Washington, D.C., to my son, John Jones." If the father no longer owns the house on Main Street at his death, the son may, depending on state law:

- receive nothing;

- receive the house into which his father moved after he sold the house on Main Street;

- be sued for title to the house by a sibling who was not named in the will because the sibling was born after the will was drafted.

One of the greatest risks with using a will or trust kit may be that the testator thinks he has a binding document.

In addition to problems of specificity, will and trust kits may also lag behind attorneys in up-dates and changes required by new legislation and new interpretations handed down by courts. Since estate law is basically different in each state, and since tax liabilities are generally determined by federal law, it is difficult for the publishers of will and trust kits to remain current in this ever-changing subject area.

Finally, one of the greatest risks in using a will or trust kit may be that the testator may think he has drafted a binding document, but the document may be declared defective or even invalid in the future when the testator dies or becomes incompetent. For example, many will kits are not designed to make the will self-proving. If a will is not self-proving, or is otherwise defective, the individual who thought he had a will may actually die intestate and the state's laws of intestate succession will control how the property is distributed.

For example, in some states, if a father and his children are killed in an accident, state law might require that a significant portion of the father's estate go to his wealthy parents rather than to his young widow who is a full-time homemaker. Similarly, if the decedent is unmarried and has no living parents, children or siblings, the laws of <u>intestate succession</u> could require distribution to a distant cousin or nephew whom the decedent barely knows, rather than to a close trusted friend to whom the decedent left everything in a self-drafted but invalid will.

Although will or trust kits offer a low cost alternative to retaining an attorney, those who use such kits run the risk that an inadvertent error may frustrate their intended disposition of property. Unfortunately, such an error may not become apparent until an individual dies, at which time it is far too late to correct it.

CHAPTER 5

The Probate Process

The Probate Process

The time for completing the probate of an estate varies depending on the jurisdiction and size of the estate.

Probate is the process by which a deceased individual's property is transferred to the persons named in his will or to the persons who otherwise inherit property under the state's law of intestate succession. Although probate is technically conducted under the supervision of the court, the majority of the work is controlled under the informal supervision of the personnel who work in the probate division of the local court. Through the clerk's office, the court ensures that all of the decedent's assets are collected, all debts are paid and all property is distributed either in accordance with the decedent's will, or if there is no will, in accordance with the state's laws of intestate succession.

Formal or Informal Probate

In most jurisdictions there are two types of probate proceedings: formal or "supervised" probate, and informal or "unsupervised" probate. The time for completing the probate of an estate varies depending on the jurisdiction and the size of the estate. It may be only three to four months or, in more complex cases, probate may be extended for several years.

Formal probate describes proceedings conducted before a judge, such as a will contest or obtaining the court's permission to sell the decedent's real property. When formal probate is utilized, all disputed matters concerning the administration of the estate are typically conducted only with the knowledge of all interested parties and the consent of the court. No formal permission is required, however, if the will specifies that the executor may sell real property without the requirement of a court order.

Informal probate, on the other hand, requires the executor to obtain permission from the court with respect to certain matters, but the majority of the executor's contact is with court personnel (such as a clerk) outside the formal courtroom setting. The executor completes his duties without the requirement of notifying all interested parties each time he wishes to complete a task on behalf of the estate. Informal probate is far more common than formal probate. Probate proceedings are administered by state courts and the rules and procedures for probate vary from state to state.

CASE IN POINT

Jane, a widow, dies leaving a written will in which she names her son Ted to serve as the Executor of her estate. In her will, Jane also states that she leaves all of her property to Ted. Prior to her death, Jane had stated to her daughters Mabel and Debra that she planned to leave all of her property to Ted, Mabel and Debra in equal shares. Mabel and Debra suspect that Ted may have used undue influence to pressure Jane to change her will so that all of her property would go to him. When Ted files Jane's will with the local probate court, Mabel and Debra may seek to have formal probate proceedings initiated so that a hearing will be conducted before a judge to determine whether Jane's will is valid. If the court rules that Jane's will is valid and that Ted did not improperly influence his mother, Jane's will may be admitted to probate and Ted will receive all of her property. If the court rules that the will is invalid, and if there are no existing original wills which Jane had previously executed, Jane's property will be distributed pursuant to her state's laws of intestate succession.

In contrast, informal probate would be utilized if neither Mabel, Debra nor any other relative challenged Jane's will.

Ted would file the original will with the probate court along with a signed oath certifying that all interested parties have been notified of his actions. If no objections are filed with the court within a specified period of time, Jane's will may be admitted to probate.

Property Subject to Probate

If a decedent owns property at the time of death, the estate must be "probated." A decedent's property may not be legally transferred outside of the probate process. (Note: It may be possible to avoid probate of many assets. See Chapter 6 for a discussion of how to avoid probate.) The requirements for initiating probate vary from state to state, but all states require that the last known will and all codicils be filed with the probate court. In many states criminal penalties may be imposed against an individual who destroys a will or fails to file an existing will. The filing requirement typically applies to formal wills and copies of formal wills. For example, where all of the decedent's property has been passed to his survivors outside of probate, such as tenancy by the entirety property, the will must still be filed.

In cases where the decedent has placed a will in a safe deposit box registered only in his name, survivors must typically obtain authority from the court to enter the box to remove and file it with the court. No further entry to the safe deposit box is generally allowed until an executor has been appointed.

Domicile — The Place for Probate

An estate is opened in most states by filing a petition for probate with the probate court in the county, city or parish where the decedent is domiciled at the time of death.

In cases where an individual is domiciled in State X and owns real property in State Y, his will would be offered for probate by the executor in State X. Depending on the laws of State Y, however, it may be necessary for the executor to initiate ancillary probate procedures in State Y whereby third parties, including the decedent's creditors in State Y, are advised of his death and of their right to file valid claims against the estate.

Domicile is defined as the jurisdiction to which an individual ultimately plans to return whenever he is absent.

Occasionally, the decedent's survivors may have a difficult time determining where a decedent was domiciled if the decedent had more than one residence. Technically, domicile is defined as the jurisdiction to which an individual ultimately plans to return whenever he is absent from that jurisdiction. For example, John Thomas, an actor, may be domiciled in New York City although he works and lives one entire year in Los Angeles. If John Thomas dies while he is in Los Angeles, his will should be probated in New York if he still considers himself domiciled in New York and ultimately plans to return there as soon as his project in Los Angeles is completed. Among the various factors the court will consider in determining whether a given jurisdiction is a decedent's place of domicile are whether the individual resides there, is registered to vote there, has a local driver's license or owns real property in the jurisdiction.

Executor/Personal Representative/ Administrator

The person named as the executor or personal representative in the will is formally appointed by the court. If a decedent died intestate, a survivor may petition the court to be named administrator of the estate. The person named as personal representative, executor or administrator all serve the same function.

He or she acts on behalf of the decedent until the estate is closed and all of the decedent's property is transferred. If the chosen personal representative declines or is unwilling to serve in that capacity, a member of the decedent's family or a friend may petition the probate court for appointment as executor. Most states have laws which establish priority in cases where more than one person seeks to be appointed executor. Many states, for example, would grant priority of appointment to the decedent's surviving spouse or adult children rather than his parents or siblings.

> **The person named as the executor in the will is formally appointed by the court.**

The Need for a Bond

Most jurisdictions require the executor to file an application for bond to protect the decedent's heirs and beneficiaries from the executor's mismanagement or other errors that could occur throughout the administration of the estate. A will may also eliminate the need for an executor to obtain a surety bond at the expense of the estate.

If a bond is required, it is usually purchased by the executor at the time he files the decedent's will with the court. Each state sets guidelines for determining the value of the bond required. This is based on numerous factors such as the relationship of the executor to the decedent, the value of the estate and the type of assets the executor will be managing.

In many jurisdictions, a representative from one or more bond companies maintains an office in the court with all necessary bond forms and applications, making it convenient for the executor to acquire a bond at the time he applies for appointment as executor.

Notification Requirements

All interested persons named in the will or otherwise entitled to receive a share of the decedent's estate must be provided with notice that the will has been filed with the court, at which time they may inspect the will at the court. This notice is usually provided by the executor at the time he files the decedent's will with the probate court and applies to be appointed executor. If the decedent has executed a self-proving will, no formal hearing is required to prove its validity.

Self-Proving Will

A <u>self-proving will</u> is one executed by the testator in the presence of the required number of witnesses and a notary public. All individuals sign the document in the presence of each other. The testator and witnesses sign a statement before the notary reflecting that they all signed the document in the presence of each other. With the use of these safeguards, it is extremely difficult for a third party to successfully challenge the validity of the document. If there is a disagreement concerning the validity of the will, however, a formal hearing will be held to determine whether it is valid.

A self-proving will is one executed by the testator in the presence of the required number of witnesses and a notary public.

If a will is not self-proving, the executor must try to locate surviving witnesses. They may be required to present either sworn testimony or an affidavit reflecting that the document presented to the court as the decedent's will is, in fact, the document which it appears to be. If the witnesses cannot be located, the court may insist on a formal hearing where other witnesses must be called to verify that the testator's signature on the will is valid and that the testator was competent on the date the will was executed.

If these elements are not proven to the court's satisfaction, it is possible that the will may not be accepted for probate and the decedent may be deemed to have died intestate. Obviously, any minor inconveniences experienced in locating a notary public and two witnesses at the time the will is executed are minimal when compared to the burdens which may be experienced by one's survivors where a will is defectively drafted or executed. *(See the forms at the end of Chapter 2 for an example of language which makes a will self-proving.)*

Other Duties of Executor

The executor must notify all of the decedent's creditors that the estate is being probated. This is usually done by publishing a notice of the decedent's death and the name and address of the person appointed as the executor. This notice is published in a local newspaper for several weeks. Creditors must file claims with the estate during a specified period of time (typically one to six months), or they are permanently barred from recovering against the estate for any debts which the decedent may have owed them.

There are many practical matters to which the executor must devote his attention. These include notifying the decedent's creditors, banks, landlords, credit card companies, and the post office that the decedent has died. All mail should be forwarded to the executor. All leases should be terminated, if possible, and utilities must be disconnected or transferred to other names. In addition, the forms at the end of this chapter include a general checklist of matters which an executor should consider during probate administration.

The executor must locate, collect and protect the decedent's assets to evaluate fully the size of the estate.

Perhaps most importantly, the personal representative must locate, collect and protect the decedent's assets to evaluate fully the size of the estate. The executor must pursue any claims which the decedent may have had against other persons. For example, if the decedent had filed a court action against a third party before he died, the executor may wish to pursue that on behalf of the decedent. Any funds recovered will be paid into the estate.

Inventories, Accounting and Tax Filing Obligations

Once the total value of the decedent's assets is determined, an inventory listing all assets and their value must be filed with the probate court. The executor then usually opens an estate checking account, through which all funds collected and paid out of the estate are managed. The executor also examines the decedent's insurance policies, pays funeral expenses, all valid debts or claims against the decedent, and prepares all income and estate or inheritance tax returns due to either the IRS or the state or local governments.

Most states require an "account" to be filed with the probate court after the executor has completed his duties. The account, which is essentially a record of the executor's transactions on behalf of the estate, includes a list of all assets acquired on behalf of the decedent, including their value. The account also lists any other property of which the executor has knowledge but which he has not collected, such as real and personal property owned by the decedent located in another jurisdiction. The account reflects all property sold or otherwise disposed of, all disbursements made, all gains and losses realized, and a schedule of distributions made, including the persons to whom and the manner in which the distribution of the estate was made.

Executor's Fees

An executor may be compensated for out-of-pocket expenses provided his request is reasonable.

At the time the account is filed, the executor typically submits an application for payment or reimbursement of his fees or out-of-pocket expenses. An executor is not required to seek compensation, and in cases where the executor is a relative or close friend of the decedent, he may decline to seek compensation. In cases where compensation is sought, most states provide that an individual will be paid provided his request is "reasonable" in view of the size of the estate and the amount of work actually performed by the executor.

Many states have guidelines, however, in determining what is reasonable. For example, a state's guidelines may suggest that from one to seven percent of the value of the gross estate is a reasonable request for compensation. An executor who requests more than seven percent may need to show compelling circumstances in order to receive more than that amount.

Attorney's Fees

Many jurisdictions require attorneys who do work related to estate administration to obtain court approval of their fees before the executor may compensate the attorney. As is the case with fee applications submitted by executors, the court will examine an attorney's application to ensure that the fee request is reasonable given the size of the estate, the value and nature of the assets, and the degree and complexity of work actually performed by the attorney.

Although a testator typically names an individual in his will whom he wishes to serve as executor, it is the executor who retains the attorney of his choice once he is appointed by the court.

It is wise for both the attorney and the executor to sign a written fee agreement at the time the attorney is retained so that both parties will have a full understanding of the fees the attorney will charge as well as the scope of the activities he or she proposes to undertake. Due to the trend in many jurisdictions to discourage the flat payment of a percentage of the decedent's estate for work performed, a typical fee agreement may provide that the attorney will be compensated at a set hourly rate, and that his or her total fee for all work performed will not exceed the greater of the total charge for the actual time expended, or a fixed percentage of the gross value of the estate, such as five to seven percent.

Closing the Estate

After the final account is approved, the executor may apply for a termination of appointment from the court. In most jurisdictions, both the executor and an attorney, if one has been retained, must apply for approval of their fees. To the extent that these applications are approved, they are paid from the estate assets as an administrative expense.

Probate procedures are specific, but vary considerably from state to state.

In summary, probate procedures are specific but vary considerably from state to state. Therefore, it is imperative that an individual consult local authorities or an attorney if he or she is administering an estate.

Matters to be Considered by an Executor During Probate Administration

Although the specific procedures to be followed vary from state to state, the following provides a broad guideline for matters which survivors frequently encounter in estate ad-ministration:

- Locate original will of the person who died.

- Open decedent's safe deposit box to review contents.

- Search for decedent's important documents and papers.

- Notify interested parties of decedent's death, including relatives and individuals named in decedent's will.

- Contact financial institutions to ensure that decedent's bank accounts are frozen.

- In the case of survivorship accounts, notify financial institution to have account name changed from joint names to surviving individual's name.

- Obtain certified copies of death certificate.

- File original will with local probate court.

- Petition court for appointment as administrator of estate where decedent has died without a will. After appointment as executor or administrator, notify all known creditors that decedent has died.

- Establish a checking account for the estate.

- Pay valid claims against the estate.

- Pay decedent's funeral expenses.

- Pay expenses of decedent's last illness.

- Contact foreign jurisdictions, i.e, other states, in which decedent owned real property to file an ancillary petition for probate.

- Locate decedent's real and personal property and safeguard all assets such as stocks, bonds, jewelry and other valuables; secure real property, taking care to protect it against vandalism, weather changes (i.e., drain the pipes), unforeseen utility cutoffs.

- File inventory with probate court reflecting all property owned by decedent on date of death.

- Check all insurance policies for coverage and expiration dates.

- Check to see if decedent is a plaintiff or defendant in any civil suit for damages, or if there are any potential claims which decedent must file before the expiration of applicable statute of limitations.

- Distribute all of decedent's property to individuals named in decedent's will.

- Prepare state and federal individual income tax returns for decedent.

- Prepare state and federal fiduciary returns for estate.

- File final accounting with court reflecting manner in which all of decedent's assets have been distributed.

PETITION FOR PROBATE

WASHINGTON LAW REPORTER FORM 600
1001 Conn. Ave.. N.W., #238, Wash., D.C. 20036-5504

Superior Court of the District of Columbia
PROBATE DIVISION
Washington, D.C. 20001

Estate of _____

Administration No. _____

_____ Age _____
Deceased

PETITION FOR PROBATE

☐ Petition for Abbreviated Probate   ☐ Petition for Standard Probate

☐ Appointment of Personal Representative   ☐ Appointment of co-Personal Representative(s) (each must sign)

☐ Appointment of Successor Personal Representative(s)   ☐ Appointment of Special Administrator(s)

The Petition of:

_____   _____
Name   Age   Address

_____   _____
Name   Age   Address

_____   _____
Name   Age   Address

hereinafter ''petitioner'' being a citizen of the United States or a lawfully admitted permanent resident thereof, of legal age, and not otherwise excluded from acting as personal representative pursuant to D.C. Code §20-303(b), shows:

    1. _____ , the decedent, a domiciliary of _____

residing at _____ died at _____
                                                                         place

on _____ (with) (without) a will.

    2. Petitioner is entitled to be appointed personal representative of the decedent's estate under D.C. Code §20-303 for the following reasons:

_____

_____

    3. The court has jurisdiction in this matter because —

    ☐ decedent died domiciled in the District of Columbia

    ☐ other—please state basis for jurisdiction _____   _____

_____

    4. There are no other proceedings regarding the administration of the estate except _____

_____

    5. The petitioner has made a diligent search for wills and codicils of the decedent, and, to the best knowledge of the petitioner the will dated

_____ and codicils dated _____

accompanying this petition (is) (are) the decedent's last will, and petitioner knows of no later will or codicil, and said will and codicil(s), if any,

came into petitioner's hands in the following manner: _____

_____

    6. All questions in this petition have been answered as required by D.C. Code §20-304(a) with the exception of the following:

_____

Form PD(25)-1183/April 93

The decedent was survived by — (please check appropriate boxes)

a. ☐ Spouse   ☐ No Spouse   Check appropriate box and go to b.

b. ☐ Children. If so, stop here; if not, go to c.

c. ☐ Grandchildren. If so, stop here; if not, go to d.

d. ☐ Parents. If so, stop here; if not, go to e.

e. ☐ Brothers and / or Sisters. If so, stop here; if not, go to f.

f. ☐ Nieces and / or Nephews. If so, stop here; if not, go to g.

g. ☐ Uncles and / or Aunts. If so, stop here; if not, go to h.

h. ☐ First cousins. If so, stop here; if not, go to i.

i. ☐ Grandparents. If so, stop here; if not, go to j.

j. ☐ Other heirs. If none, go to k.

k. ☐ Notify Office of the Corporation Counsel, Special Litigation Section.
1 Judiciary Square, 441 4th Street, N.W., 6th Floor, Washington, D.C. 20001.

Indicate, when applicable, grandchildren and nieces and nephews by family groups, by showing the name of their deceased parent who was related to the decedent.

LIST OF INTERESTED PERSONS must include names of heirs if decedent died intestate; heirs and legatees, including trustees and all named Personal Representatives if the decedent died testate. Refer to D.C. Code §19-301 through 312 and §20-101(d)(1). Add additional sheets, if needed. **Note:** If each trustee is also a petitioning party or acting personal representative, list all beneficiaries under trust. Refer to D.C. Code §20-101(g).

For minors 15 and under, notice may be served on custodian only. For those 16 and above, notice must be served on minor and custodian.

Name of Heir / Legatee / Personal Representative	Address	Relationship

WITNESSES TO WILLS / CODICILS (Names)

(List the name, address and relationship of each heir at law and next of kin, and whether any of them is under any legal disability, the name and address of the guardian, conservator, committee or custodian of any such person who is under a legal disability, and, if any such heir at law and next of kin is an infant, the date of birth, and the name of the custodian of any who is under 16 years of age.)

Character, Location and Estimated Value of Property titled in decedent's name:

Estimated Value

Real Property located in the District of Columbia

Total $

Personal Property located in the District of Columbia and other jurisdictions

Total $

Debts, Funeral Expenses, Inheritance Taxes

Debts secured (*i.e.*, mortgages, tax liens, etc.) :

Total $

Debts unsecured (*i.e.*, medical bills, credit card bills, utility bills, etc.) :

Total $

Funeral Expenses:

☐ Paid by _____
name

Total $

☐ Unpaid

Total $

Inheritance taxes, *if the decedent died prior to April 1, 1987*
only on personal property under control of personal representative

Total $

-4-

WHEREFORE, the petitioner prays that letters be granted appointing petitioner personal representative(s) of the decedent's estate in (abbreviated) (standard) probate proceeding, and that the will dated _____ and codicil(s) dated _____ _____ be admitted to probate and record, and that the additional relief be granted:

_____ .

DECLARATION OF PETITIONER

I do solemnly declare and affirm under the penalty of law that the contents of the foregoing petition are true and correct to the best of my knowledge. information and belief.

☐ I am a member of the D.C. bar and hereby guarantee court costs.

_____   _____
Signature of Attorney for Petitioner   Signature of Petitioner   (Tel. No.)

_____   _____
Typed Name of Attorney   Signature of Petitioner   (Tel. No.)

_____
Signature of Petitioner   (Tel. No.)

_____   _____   _____
Attorney's Address   Telephone No.   Unified Bar No.

ACCEPTANCE AND CONSENT OF EACH PERSONAL REPRESENTATIVE

I do hereby accept the duties of the office of personal representative of the estate of _____ , deceased, and consent to personal jurisdiction in any action brought in the District of Columbia against me as personal representative or arising out of the duties of the office of personal representative pursuant to D.C. Code §20-501.

_____   _____   _____
Signature of Petitioner   Signature of Petitioner   Signature of Petitioner

POWER OF ATTORNEY

To be Executed By Each Non-resident Personal Representative

Pursuant to D.C. Code §20-303(b)(7), I do hereby irrevocably appoint the Register and successors in office as the person upon whom all notices and process issued by a competent court in the District of Columbia may be served with the same effect as personal service in relation to all suits or matters pertaining to the estate in which the letters are to issue.

_____   _____
(Name)   (Address)

_____   _____
(Name)   (Address)

_____   _____
(Name)   (Address)

CHAPTER 6

How To Avoid Probate

How to Avoid Probate

A goal in many estate plans is either to avoid probate entirely or at least to minimize the assets subject to the probate process. The reasons most frequently offered for wishing to avoid probate include delay, cost and the publicity associated with the probate process.

Drawbacks of Probate

Probate is a court supervised proceeding. The delays that are a part of any court proceeding may be part of the probate process. It is not unusual for the probate of a relatively simple estate to take more than six months.

Any filing made with the probate court is generally a matter of public record. Probate filings describe the nature and extent of a decedent's assets and how the decedent disposed of his assets. Although probate filings are not typically publicized, they are generally available for public inspection.

A third frequently cited disadvantage of probate is the cost associated with it. The costs involved may include attorney's and personal representative's fees, as well as the costs that may be imposed by the court, such as filing fees or costs of necessary appraisers.

Will Substitutes

The only way to avoid probate is to ensure that upon death there are no probate assets.

The only sure way to avoid probate is to take steps to ensure that upon death there are no probate assets. Probate assets are those assets that may be transferred only through the probate process. Prudent planning may permit a person to take steps to avoid or minimize the assets subject to probate by using a will substitute.

As the name suggests, a will substitute is a planning technique that permits a person to transfer property at death without using a will. It permits property to pass to the intended beneficiary without going through the probate process. It serves the purpose of a will, but it is not a will. The most common will substitutes are assets owned with a right of survivorship, property that passes by contract, and property held in a revocable living trust.

Property Passing by Operation of Law

If property is owned either in a <u>joint tenancy with a right of survivorship</u> or in a <u>tenancy by the entirety,</u> it passes to the surviving tenant upon the death of the first tenant by operation of law. (See Chapter 1 for a discussion of property which passes by operation of law.)

A house is the most significant asset in many estates. It is frequently owned with a spouse or other related party in either a tenancy by the entirety or in a joint tenancy. Under either of these forms of ownership, the house passes to the survivor by operation of law and is not subject to probate. The ownership of bank accounts, mutual funds, brokerage accounts and such items of personal property as an automobile may also be structured to permit the property to pass to the surviving tenant by operation of law. If the property is owned in a <u>survivorship account,</u> it is not subject to probate upon the death of the first tenant.

If property is owned in a survivorship, it is not subject to probate upon the death of the first tenant.

Property Passing by Contract

Property governed by contract may also pass outside of the probate process. Common examples of such assets include life insurance proceeds, pension plan assets, and annuities.

A life insurance policy is a contract between the insured and the insurance company. The insurance company has a contractual obligation to pay any policy proceeds to the named beneficiary upon the death of the insured. Similarly, annuities typically contain a provision that specifies that the company paying the annuity is obligated to pay any proceeds to a designated beneficiary upon the death of the annuity owner.

Most pension plans also require a plan participant to designate a beneficiary. In the event of the death of the plan participant, the plan administrator is obligated to pay all funds in the decedent's account to the designated beneficiary.

Property which passes by contract is discussed in Chapter 1.

Revocable Living Trusts

A third common will substitute is a revocable living trust. It is perhaps one of the most widely publicized devices for avoiding probate. The structure, uses, advantages and disadvantages of a revocable living trust are discussed in detail in Chapter 12.

Use of a Pour-Over Will

It is generally advisable to use a pour-over will in conjunction with one or more will substitutes. A pour-over will ensures that property is distributed in accordance with a decedent's wishes. It is a standby device that will only be used if the decedent owns any property at the time of death that does not pass to the intended beneficiary through the use of a will substitute. Typically, a pour-over will provides that all of the decedent's property will pass either to a specifically named person, such as a spouse, or to a trust.

It is generally advisable to use a pour-over will in conjunction with one or more will substitutes.

The provisions of the trust will specify how the property is to be distributed to any beneficiaries.

If a person relies on one or more will substitutes to pass all property, but neglects to take the action necessary to ensure that the will substitute will be effective, this property would pass under the laws of intestate succession. A pour-over will prevents this from happening.

Any property that passes under a pour-over will is subject to probate. Presumably, the amount of such property would be limited and probate could be handled more quickly.

CASE IN POINT

Jim Carney died unexpectedly at age 57. Among the assets passing to his wife Jill, age 56, were the proceeds of a $500,000 life insurance policy. Jill elected to take the life insurance proceeds in the form of an annuity. The insurance policy provided that she would receive a monthly annuity for life. The full value of any funds in the account at the time of her death would be paid either to her estate or to a designated beneficiary. She filed the insurance papers shortly after Jim's death, when she was still emotionally upset. She simply checked the box designating her estate as beneficiary.

In Jill's case, the contract (i.e., the annuity) required any proceeds to be paid to her estate. These proceeds ultimately will be subject to probate because they will not be paid to a designated beneficiary. If Jill does not have a will designating the recipient of these funds, they will be distributed in accordance with the laws of intestate succession in the state of her domicile. Use of a pour-over will would avoid this result.

Avoiding Probate May Not Work for Everyone

While avoiding probate may be a desirable objective, it may not make sense in all instances. The property transfers required to make a will substitute effective may not be practical because the tax costs associated with transferring property may be unacceptably high in some states. Moreover, persons who have a gross estate in excess of $600,000 may be required to incur other unacceptable tax burdens in an effort to avoid probate.

Avoiding probate may not make sense in all instances.

CASE IN POINT

Transfer Tax

Margaret Horton lives in a house in the fashionable Georgetown section of Washington, D.C. She and her deceased husband bought the house for $30,000 in the late 1940s and it is now worth $800,000. Margaret wants to prepare a revocable living trust and transfer all of her assets to it, including her house. While Margaret may transfer her house to the trust, she must do so by preparing a new deed that reflects the trust as the owner of the property. This deed must be filed with the D.C. Recorder of Deeds. No transfer tax will be imposed upon the fair market value of the property at the time of transfer since Margaret, as grantor, is also the sole beneficiary of the trust. Most states now exempt transfers of this nature from transfer tax.

Income/Gift Tax

Arthur and Harriet Wilson bought their house as tenants by the entirety in 1957.

When Arthur died in 1970, Harriet became the sole owner of the house because she was the surviving tenant. She wants to transfer the house to her daughter, Allison, because she wants to avoid having the house pass through probate.

Harriet's basis in the house is $40,000; it is now worth $180,000. There is no transfer tax in Harriet's home state. Although Harriet may transfer her house to Allison this may have unintended income and gift tax consequences. If she makes the transfer it will be a taxable gift. If she has previously used her unified credit, she may be required to pay a gift tax. When Allison receives the gift, her basis in the house will be a carry-over basis of $40,000.

If, when her mother dies, she sells the house for $180,000, she will have a taxable gain of $140,000. If she is in the 33 percent federal and state tax bracket, she will have a federal tax liability of $46,200. If her mother had simply retained title to the house and passed it to Allison through the probate process, Allison would have a stepped-up basis of $180,000 and no tax would be due upon the sale of the house. (See discussion of stepped-up basis and carry-over basis in Chapter 7.)

While Harriet may be able to accomplish her goal of avoiding probate, the costs of doing so would be significant.

Conclusion

Avoiding probate is certainly something to be considered as part of the planning process. The key, however, is that avoiding probate must be part of an overall estate plan. It should not be a goal to be achieved at all costs.

Avoiding probate should not be a goal to be achieved at all costs.

CHAPTER 7

Federal Estate and Gift Taxes

Federal Estate and Gift Taxes

NOTE: At the time of publication of this 4th edition, a number of significant changes to the estate and gift tax laws were being considered by Congress. This edition does not reflect any tax law changes made after 1996.

The prudent use of a will or trust as estate planning tools can result in tax savings during one's lifetime. Their use also ensures that assets will be distributed in accordance with the individual's wishes at death.

Proper use of these tools requires an understanding of their tax consequences. While tax considerations alone should not dictate any individual's estate plan, an effective estate plan should accomplish an individual's objectives in a way that minimizes the amount of taxes that must be paid.

The use of a will or trust requires an understanding of their tax consequences.

Implementation of any estate plan necessarily involves transfers of property either during life or at death. These transfers may result in an estate or a gift tax liability. The federal estate and gift tax are unified transfer taxes.[3] They impose a tax upon the transfer of property either during life (the gift tax) or at death (the estate tax).

The transfer tax is graduated. It varies from a low of 18 percent on taxable transfers of less than $10,000 to a high of 55 percent on taxable transfers in excess of $3 million. *As a result of a number of significant changes implemented as part of the Tax Reform Act of 1976, many middle income individuals may completely avoid any estate or gift tax liability.*

If an individual's total net worth is less than $600,000, he may never have a transfer tax liability. The principles discussed in this chapter may be of particular interest to individuals whose net worth exceeds $600,000.

As a result of the increased prevalence of dual income households, the rising costs of homes, and the presence of life insurance, many couples who do not consider themselves wealthy may be surprised to discover that their joint net worth exceeds $600,000. Such individuals should have at least a basic understanding of the transfer tax.

---

[3] Prior to 1976 there were separate federal estate and gift taxes. The Tax Reform Act of 1976 replaced the separate estate and gift taxes with one unified transfer tax.

Relationship to Income Tax

The transfer tax and the income tax are two entirely different taxes. An income tax liability applies only to income and the transfer tax is imposed on transfers of property by gift during life or after death. Any money or property received either by gift or inheritance is not subject to income tax but may be subject to transfer tax.

The Gift Tax

The gift tax applies to any taxable gift. The person making the gift, the donor, is the person obligated to pay this tax. Several liberal provisions of the federal transfer tax make it possible for most persons to avoid any gift tax liability. These provisions include the unlimited <u>marital deduction</u> for any gifts to a spouse, the <u>annual gift tax exclusion,</u> the <u>split gift election</u> and the <u>unified transfer tax credit.</u>

Any money or property received either by gift or inheritance is not subject to income tax but may be subject to transfer tax.

The Marital Deduction

All gifts to a spouse are fully deductible. As such, no gift tax liability arises from such gifts, regardless of their value. It is generally not necessary to file a gift tax return for gifts to a spouse.

Annual Gift Tax Exclusion

The second tax provision that permits the avoidance of gift tax liability is the $10,000 annual gift tax exclusion. This exclusion applies on a per donee basis.

This means that an individual may make an unlimited number of gifts without incurring a gift tax liability provided the total value of any gift(s) to one individual does not exceed $10,000 in any one calendar year. A gift must be one of a <u>present interest</u> in order to qualify for the annual exclusion. This means that the donee, or recipient, of the gift must have an immediate right to take the gift at the time it is made. In contrast, a gift of a <u>future interest</u> is one to which the donee's right to receive the gift is postponed until the occurrence of a definite or contingent event in the future. Gifts of a future interest generally do not qualify for the $10,000 annual exclusion.

CASE IN POINT

Present Interest

Terry decides to make a gift of $1,000 to his grandson Bob when Bob graduates from medical school. He sends Bob a check for $1,000 which Bob cashes immediately, thanking his grandfather for the gift.

Terry has given Bob a gift of a present interest which is not subject to the gift tax because it does not exceed $10,000.

Future Interest

Assume for purposes of the example above that Terry decides to make a gift of $1,000 to Bob prior to his graduation, but that Terry does not want Bob to receive the gift until he either successfully completes medical school or reaches age 25. Terry writes a letter to Bob advising him that he has deposited $1,000 in a bank account and that Bob may collect the $1,000 either when he graduates from medical school or reaches age 25. Because Bob does not have a present right to receive the $1,000, the gift is one of a future interest. Thus, Terry's gift does not qualify for the annual gift tax exclusion.

The Split Gift Election

The $10,000 annual exclusion permits a husband and wife to make tax-free gifts of $20,000 per year to any one individual through the use of what is known as the <u>split gift election.</u> The split gift election is only available to married couples. Thus, if a husband and wife have four children they may make total annual gifts to their children of $80,000 without incurring any gift tax liability.

If the value of any gifts to one individual exceed $10,000 in a calendar year, the donor will be required to file a gift tax return. The gift tax return is an annual return and it must be filed between January 1st and April 15th of the year following the calendar year when the gifts were made. The filing of a tax return, however, does not mean that the donor will be required to pay any gift tax.

CASE IN POINT

Frank Lane has inherited $250,000 from his recently deceased father. He and his wife Marian agree that they do not need all of this money and that they would like to make gifts of $20,000 to each of their five adult children. They make the gifts on September 15, 1997.

Although the gift will be made solely from Frank's individual property, any gift tax may be avoided if Marian and Frank agree to make a split gift election. That is, they agree to treat each $20,000 gift as if it were made one-half by Frank and one-half by Marian. They must file a gift tax return to make this election even though there will be no gift tax liability. This return must be signed by both of them and must be filed by April 15, 1998.

Gifts for Educational or Medical Expenses

An unlimited gift tax exclusion is allowed for the payment of an individual's educational or medical expenses. Educational expenses include tuition, but not room, board or books. Only those medical expenses that are not reimbursed by insurance qualify for exclusion. Payment must be made directly to the educational or medical institution by the donor.

Payment must be made directly to the educational or medical institution by the donor.

Payment of educational or medical expenses does not count against the $10,000 annual exclusion.

CASE IN POINT

Harriet's grandson, Joe, has been accepted to medical school and his tuition for the first year is $25,000. While driving to school Joe was involved in an accident and was injured. His insurance did not cover his $3,000 in medical expenses. Harriet pays Joe's tuition directly to his medical school and also pays his medical expenses directly to the hospital where he received treatment. Payment of Joe's tuition and his medical expenses are not counted as gifts. If Harriet chooses to do so, she may also make a gift of $10,000 to Joe during the current tax year.

If Harriet gives Joe $25,000 to pay his tuition, she is not entitled to claim the educational expense exclusion. Rather, she will be treated as having made a $15,000 taxable gift (i.e. $25,000 minus her $10,000 annual exclusion).

Unified Transfer Tax Credit

The "unified credit" allows a donor to give away $600,000 tax-free during his lifetime.

If there is a gift tax liability, a <u>unified credit</u> is available to offset this liability. This "unified credit" allows a donor to give away a total of $600,000 tax-free during his lifetime. If all of an individual's combined taxable gifts total less than $600,000 (or less than $1.2 million for each couple), this credit eliminates any gift tax liability. Further, if all or any portion of the credit remains unused during an individual's life, the remaining portion may be used as a credit against federal estate taxes.

Filing the Gift Tax Return

A gift tax return must be filed for any calendar year in which a gift is made unless the gift is to a spouse and the marital deduction applies, or if it qualifies for the $10,000 annual exclusion.

The return is due on or before April 15, following the close of the calendar year in which the gift is made. Extensions of up to six months may be granted by the IRS. If any tax is due, it must be paid at the time of filing the return. The first page of the federal gift tax return appears at the end of this chapter.

The Federal Estate Tax

The federal estate tax is imposed on any property owned by the decedent at the time of death. The determination of whether an individual has an estate tax liability must begin with the computation of the gross estate. An individual's <u>gross estate</u> includes all property in which the decedent had an interest at the time of his death including:

Compute the gross estate to determine whether an individual has an estate tax liability.

- any property owned by the decedent at the time of death;

- any property over which the decedent retained control at the time of death;

- the proceeds of any life insurance policy owned by the decedent at the time of death;

- the value of the decedent's interest in any jointly held property. If property is held in a joint tenancy or in a tenancy by the entirety, it will be presumed that one-half of the value of the property is includable in the estate of the decedent;

- any property the decedent transferred over which he retained a right of control at the time of his death.

CASE IN POINT

David Riley is a 63-year-old man who has been married to his wife, Mary, for 35 years. David and Mary own a home in suburban Washington, D.C. This home is owned in a tenancy by the entirety and is worth approximately $300,000. The house has a mortgage of $125,000. In addition, David was the recipient of $250,000 in insurance proceeds at the time of his father's death. He and Mary made a gift of $100,000 of these proceeds to their children in September, 1990, and David retained the remaining $150,000 in a certificate of deposit in his name. David also owns a $350,000 life insurance policy and Mary is the beneficiary of the policy. David and Mary jointly own miscellaneous assets including stocks, bonds, mutual funds and bank accounts, worth $100,000. Finally, they also jointly own various personal effects such as furniture and automobiles worth about $30,000.

David's other personal effects, such as clothing, are worth about $5,000. David's gross estate would be computed as follows:

Jointly Owned Property —David's One-Half Interest

Family Residence $150,000
Stocks, bonds, etc. 50,000
Furniture and autos 15,000
David's share of joint gift to children, less $10,000 annual exclusion 30,000*

David's one-half of jointly owned property $245,000

David's Separate Property
Certificates of Deposit 150,000
Personal Effects 5,000
Life Insurance Policy Proceeds 350,000

David's Separate Property $505,000
TOTAL Value of David's Gross Estate $750,000

*Total value of joint gift from David and Mary to their children was $100,000. One-half of this amount, i.e., $50,000 is included in David's gross estate. He may take a $10,000 annual exclusion of the amount of the gift to each child. Since David and Mary have two children, he may exclude $10,000 of the gift for each child, or $20,000.

All of David's property is now left to his wife Mary in his will. If the value of David's estate remains the same, his executor would be required to file a federal estate tax return, but no tax would be payable because of the marital deduction. David and Mary may wish to consider using a bypass trust to avoid any tax liability on either of their estates. (See Chapter 15 for a discussion of this technique.)

Valuation of Estate

The decedent's gross estate may be valued either on the date of death or on the alternate valuation date. The alternate valuation date is the date six months after the date of death. If the alternate valuation date is selected, all of the decedent's property must be valued as of that date. The law does not allow the estate to value some assets on the date of death and other assets on the alternate valuation date.

CASE IN POINT

John Smith died on June 5, 1987. At that time, he owned stocks, bonds and mutual funds worth $700,000, a parcel of undeveloped real estate located in an area 75 miles outside of New York City worth $200,000, and other assets worth approximately $300,000. The total value of John's assets on the date of his death was $1,200,000.00.

After John's death, two significant events occurred: the stock market declined substantially in October, 1987 and John's stock holdings declined in value to $500,000. In addition, John's executor learned that a major company announced that it planned to build a large facility on a 1,000-acre parcel which included John's real estate. Company representatives approached John's executor and offered to pay $450,000 for the property. As a result of these two events, the value of John's estate as of December 5, 1987 (the alternate valuation date) was $1,250,000. In this situation, it would be in the estate's best interest to value John's estate as of the date of John's death.

The valuation date must be selected carefully with the goal of keeping the size of the estate as low as possible, and it must be selected when the estate tax return is filed.

Estate Tax Liability

The executor, personal representative or administrator of the estate is required to file a federal estate tax return if the gross estate exceeds $600,000. A return must be filed even if the estate has no tax liability. The first page of the federal estate tax return appears at the end of this chapter.

A federal estate tax return must be filed if the gross estate exceeds $600,000.

Deductions

A number of deductions may be claimed on the federal estate tax return that decrease the size of the estate. These deductions include debts or obligations owed by the decedent at the time of death (i.e., a mortgage); administrative expenses, such as court costs or attorney's fees; funeral expenses; medical expenses associated with the final illness; any charitable bequests, and the most significant of all, the marital deduction.

CASE IN POINT

In the case of David Riley described earlier, David's gross estate is $750,000. Accordingly, his estate will be required to file an estate tax return. His taxable estate, however, is zero (0) and is computed as follows:

Gross Estate	$750,000
Deductions	
Debts	-60,000
Administrative Expenses	-30,000
Adjusted Gross Estate..	$660,000
Marital Deduction	-630,000*
Taxable Estate	$30,000
No estate tax due on this amount	

*David's estate takes a marital deduction for the full value of the property which is transferred from his estate to Mary's estate at the time of his death. The total value of David's estate ($660,000) passes to Mary with the exception of the $30,000 gift he made to his children.

No estate tax will be payable if he has not used the full amount of his unified credit.

The Marital Deduction

An estate is entitled to a deduction equal to the value of any property which passes to the decedent's surviving spouse. As a consequence, federal estate tax liability may be entirely avoided by having all property pass to the surviving spouse.

While it is always possible to avoid estate tax on the first estate of a married couple to die, this is not always the wisest course to follow. The surviving spouse may not need all of this property. When the surviving spouse subsequently dies, the value of his/her estate may be so high because of the inherited property that it results in a tax that is higher than would have been paid if the surviving spouse had not inherited all of the property originally.

Accordingly, if a surviving spouse has substantial assets and does not need all of the decedent's assets, it may be wise to bequeath property to someone other than the surviving spouse, since one of the goals of effective estate planning is to ensure that a husband and wife pay the least aggregate amount of federal estate tax possible.

CASE IN POINT

Stephen and Suzanne Thompson have a combined net worth of $1.8 million. Of this amount, $1 million would be includable in Stephen's gross estate and the remaining $800,000 would be includable in Suzanne's gross estate. Under Stephen's will, Suzanne will receive $400,000 outright and the remaining $600,000 will be placed in a bypass trust. (See Chapter 15 for a discussion of a bypass trust.) The trustee is directed to pay all trust income to Suzanne during her lifetime. She would also have the right to request to be paid up to 5 percent of the trust principal annually. In addition, the trustee has the discretion to make annual distributions of principal to Suzanne to pay any medical bills or any unusual expenses.

The tax savings of this plan may be illustrated as follows:

	At Stephen's Death With Bypass Trust	W/O	At Suzanne's Death With Bypass Trust	W/O
Gross Estate	1,000,000	1,000,000	1,200,000*	1,800,000
Marital Deduction	- 400,000	-1,000,000	0	0
Taxable Estate	600,000	0	1,200,000	1,800,000
Tax	192,800	0	427,800	690,800
Unified Credit	-192,800	0	-192,800	-192,800
Tax Due	0	0	235,000	498,000

*This figure is the total of Suzanne's property ($800,000) plus the $400,000 she receives under Stephen's will.

This planning technique protects Suzanne because she has the right to all of the income from the trust. In addition, the trustee has the discretion to provide additional funds if Suzanne incurs unforeseen problems requiring substantial funds. It illustrates that prudent use of the martial deduction can result in substantial tax savings. Without a bypass trust, a total of $498,000 in federal estate taxes must be paid. With a bypass trust, however, the total federal estate tax paid by this couple is $235,000, resulting in savings of $263,000.

Filing/Paying the Federal Estate Tax

The federal estate tax return is filed on Internal Revenue Service Form 706 and is due nine (9) months after the date of death. If any federal estate tax is payable, it must be paid at time of filing.[4] Remember, once the tax liability is computed, any unused portion of the unified credit may be used to offset any remaining liability. If no portion of the unified credit has been used to offset any gift tax, no federal estate tax is payable on any taxable estate of less than $600,000.

If any federal estate tax is payable, it must be paid at time of filing.

If the estate is large, however, and the resulting estate tax may amount to thousands of dollars, the executor often must liquidate assets in order to pay the tax. This requires the executor to maximize estate assets so that sales are conducted at the highest possible value and so that assets likely to appreciate are not sold simply to pay estate taxes.

The financial sophistication necessary to manage the assets of a large estate, plus the fact that the federal estate tax return is considerably more complex than the federal income tax return, usually requires executors of large estates to seek professional assistance. Because of the generous estate and gift tax deductions, however, most middle income individuals can avoid all estate or gift tax liability if they plan properly and seek professional assistance during the planning process.

---

[4] In certain instances the tax laws provided that the estate tax may be paid in installments over a period of up to 10 years. This is only permissible, however, if the major portion of the estate is either an interest in a closely held business or a farm. An individual in this situation should seek professional assistance.

State Taxes

In planning projected tax liabilities, the reader should be cautioned that many states impose transfer taxes which could reduce the assets of the estate or which must be paid by the recipient of a gift. Some states impose inheritance taxes upon recipients of property for the "privilege" of receiving the property. Other states may impose estate taxes upon the donor of property as a means of taxing the "privilege" of transferring wealth from one individual to another. Many states have a credit tax that may be used to offset federal estate taxes. Since these laws vary greatly from state to state, it is essential to consult a local tax advisor or attorney to ascertain whether the local law imposes these transfer and estate taxes.

Since laws vary greatly from state to state, it is essential to consult a local tax advisor or attorney.

Income Tax Concerns/Stepped-up Basis

The preceding discussion illustrates that if a decedent owns property at the time of death, his estate may realize a significant income tax benefit if the property appreciated between the time the decedent acquired it and the time of his death.

Under the income tax laws, taxable gain is the difference between the purchase price of an asset and the sales price of the asset. For example, if Linda bought 100 shares of stock for $1,000 and sold them for $1,500, her taxable gain would be $500, or the difference between the purchase price and the sales price. The reference point for determining gain or loss is the basis of an asset. If a person purchases an asset, its basis is the cost of the asset.

If a person receives an asset by gift, the basis is a carry-over basis. This means that the basis of the gift property "carries over" from the person making the gift, the donor, to the person receiving it, the donee. For example, if Linda gives 100 shares of stock which she purchased for $1,000 to her daughter Kris, Linda's basis of $1,000 carries over to Kris. If Kris then sells the stock for $1,500, she will have a taxable gain of $500.

If a person inherits property, (e.g., land, houses, stocks, bonds, etc.), the basis of the property is <u>stepped-up</u> to its fair market value at the date of death. If an asset has appreciated, the amount of appreciation escapes income taxation. For example, if Agnes Archer's will provides that her son Jim will inherit her house, Jim's basis in the house will be a <u>stepped-up basis.</u> His basis will be the fair market value of the house at his mother's death. If Agnes purchased her house for $40,000 in 1960, but is was worth $200,000 at the time of her death, Jim's basis will be $200,000.

CASE IN POINT

During his 40 years of employment with IBM, Joe Vincent purchased 1,000 shares of stock in IBM under the company's stock purchase plan for a total cost of $30,000. Joe's basis in the IBM stock is its cost, or $30,000. Joe is now financially comfortable and does not need the income from the stock, now worth $100,000. He is considering making a gift of this stock to his son Joe, Jr. Alternatively, he may keep the stock and make a gift of cash to Joe, Jr.

If Joe makes a gift to his son, his basis of $30,000 will carry over. Thus, if Joe Jr. sells this stock for $100,000, he will have a taxable gain of $70,000. If he is in the combined 33 percent federal/state tax bracket, a tax of $23,100 will be payable on this gain. If Joe retains the stock until he dies and gives it to his son under his will, Joe Jr. will get a stepped-up basis equal to the fair market value of the stock at the date of his father's death. If it is worth $100,000 at Joe's death, Joe Jr.'s basis in the inherited stock will be $100,000. If he sells the stock for $100,000 he will have no taxable gain.

The income tax benefits available from use of the stepped-up basis provisions of the tax law indicate the advisability of passing appreciated property to your loved ones at death rather than by gift.

Unified Transfer Tax Rates for 1994 and Thereafter

Table A — Unifed Rate Schedule

Column A	Column B	Column C	Column D
Taxable amount over	Taxable amount not over	Tax on amount in Column A	Rate of tax on excess over amount in Column A
			Percent
$ 0	$ 10,000	$ 0	18
10,000	20,000	1,800	20
20,000	40,000	3,800	22
40,000	60,000	8,200	24
60,000	80,000	13,000	26
80,000	150,000	18,200	28
150,000	250,000	38,800	32
250,000	500,000	70,800	34
500,000	750,000	155,800	37
750,000	1,000,000	248,300	39
1,000,000	1,250,000	345,800	41
1,250,000	1,500,000	448,300	43
1,500,000	2,000,000	555,800	45
2,000,000	2,500,000	780,800	49
2,500,000	3,000,000	1,025,800	53
3,000,000	------------	1,290,800	55

Form **706**
(Rev. April 1997)

Department of the Treasury
Internal Revenue Service

United States Estate (and Generation-Skipping Transfer) Tax Return

Estate of a citizen or resident of the United States (see separate instructions). To be filed for decedents dying after October 8, 1990. For Paperwork Reduction Act Notice, see page 1 of the separate instructions.

OMB No. 1545-0015

Part 1.—Decedent and Executor

1a Decedent's first name and middle initial (and maiden name, if any)	**1b** Decedent's last name
	2 Decedent's social security no.
3a Legal residence (domicile) at time of death (county, state, and ZIP code, or foreign country)	**3b** Year domicile established **4** Date of birth **5** Date of death
6a Name of executor (see page 2 of the instructions)	**6b** Executor's address (number and street including apartment or suite no. or rural route; city, town, or post office; state; and ZIP code)
6c Executor's social security number (see page 2 of the instructions)	
7a Name and location of court where will was probated or estate administered	**7b** Case number

8 If decedent died testate, check here ▶ ☐ and attach a certified copy of the will. **9** If Form 4768 is attached, check here ▶ ☐

10 If Schedule R-1 is attached, check here ▶ ☐

Part 2.—Tax Computation

1 Total gross estate (from Part 5, Recapitulation, page 3, item 10)		**1**	
2 Total allowable deductions (from Part 5, Recapitulation, page 3, item 20) . . .		**2**	
3 Taxable estate (subtract line 2 from line 1)		**3**	
4 Adjusted taxable gifts (total taxable gifts (within the meaning of section 2503) made by the decedent after December 31, 1976, other than gifts that are includible in decedent's gross estate (section 2001(b)))		**4**	
5 Add lines 3 and 4		**5**	
6 Tentative tax on the amount on line 5 from Table A on page 10 of the instructions		**6**	
7a If line 5 exceeds $10,000,000, enter the lesser of line 5 or $21,040,000. If line 5 is $10,000,000 or less, skip lines 7a and 7b and enter -0- on line 7c .	**7a**		
b Subtract $10,000,000 from line 7a	**7b**		
c Enter 5% (.05) of line 7b		**7c**	
8 Total tentative tax (add lines 6 and 7c)		**8**	
9 Total gift tax payable with respect to gifts made by the decedent after December 31, 1976. Include gift taxes by the decedent's spouse for such spouse's share of split gifts (section 2513) only if the decedent was the donor of these gifts and they are includible in the decedent's gross estate (see instructions)		**9**	
10 Gross estate tax (subtract line 9 from line 8)		**10**	
11 Maximum unified credit against estate tax	**11**	192,800 00	
12 Adjustment to unified credit. (This adjustment may not exceed $6,000. See page 7 of the instructions.)	**12**		
13 Allowable unified credit (subtract line 12 from line 11)		**13**	
14 Subtract line 13 from line 10 (but do not enter less than zero)		**14**	
15 Credit for state death taxes. Do not enter more than line 14. Figure the credit by using the amount on line 3 less $60,000. See Table B in the instructions and **attach credit evidence** (see instructions) .		**15**	
16 Subtract line 15 from line 14		**16**	
17 Credit for Federal gift taxes on pre-1977 gifts (section 2012) (attach computation)	**17**		
18 Credit for foreign death taxes (from Schedule(s) P). (Attach Form(s) 706-CE.)	**18**		
19 Credit for tax on prior transfers (from Schedule Q)	**19**		
20 Total (add lines 17, 18, and 19)		**20**	
21 Net estate tax (subtract line 20 from line 16)		**21**	
22 Generation-skipping transfer taxes (from Schedule R, Part 2, line 10)		**22**	
23 Section 4980A increased estate tax (from Schedule S, Part I, line 17) (see page 20 of the instructions)		**23**	
24 Total transfer taxes (add lines 21, 22, and 23)		**24**	
25 Prior payments. Explain in an attached statement	**25**		
26 United States Treasury bonds redeemed in payment of estate tax .	**26**		
27 Total (add lines 25 and 26).		**27**	
28 Balance due (or overpayment) (subtract line 27 from line 24).		**28**	

Under penalties of perjury, I declare that I have examined this return, including accompanying schedules and statements, and to the best of my knowledge and belief, it is true, correct, and complete. Declaration of preparer other than the executor is based on all information of which preparer has any knowledge.

Signature(s) of executor(s) _____ Date _____

Signature of preparer other than executor _____ Address (and ZIP code) _____ Date _____

Cat. No. 20548R

5/12/97   Published by Tax Management Inc., a Subsidiary of The Bureau of National Affairs, Inc.   706.1

Form 709
(Rev. December 1996)

Department of the Treasury
Internal Revenue Service

United States Gift (and Generation-Skipping Transfer) Tax Return

(Section 6019 of the Internal Revenue Code) (For gifts made after December 31, 1991)

Calendar year 19 ....

▶ See separate instructions. For Privacy Act Notice, see the instructions for Form 1040.

OMB No. 1545-0020

Part 1—General Information

1 Donor's first name and middle initial	2 Donor's last name	3 Donor's social security number
4 Address (number, street, and apartment number)		5 Legal residence (domicile) (county and state)
6 City, state, and ZIP code		7 Citizenship

		Yes	No
8	If the donor died during the year, check here ▶ ☐ and enter date of death.............. , ...		
9	If you received an extension of time to file this Form 709, check here ▶ ☐ and attach the Form 4868, 2688, 2350, or extension letter		
10	Enter the total number of separate donees listed on Schedule A—count each person only once. ▶		
11a	Have you (the donor) previously filed a Form 709 (or 709-A) for any other year? If the answer is "No," do not complete line 11b .		
11b	If the answer to line 11a is "Yes," has your address changed since you last filed Form 709 (or 709-A)?		
12	Gifts by husband or wife to third parties.—Do you consent to have the gifts (including generation-skipping transfers) made by you and by your spouse to third parties during the calendar year considered as made one-half by each of you? (See instructions.) (If the answer is "Yes," the following information must be furnished and your spouse must sign the consent shown below. If the answer is "No," skip lines 13–18 and go to Schedule A.)		
13	Name of consenting spouse	14 SSN	
15	Were you married to one another during the entire calendar year? (see instructions)		
16	If the answer to 15 is "No," check whether ☐ married ☐ divorced or ☐ widowed, and give date (see instructions) ▶		
17	Will a gift tax return for this calendar year be filed by your spouse?		
18	Consent of Spouse—I consent to have the gifts (and generation-skipping transfers) made by me and by my spouse to third parties during the calendar year considered as made one-half by each of us. We are both aware of the joint and several liability for tax created by the execution of this consent.		

Consenting spouse's signature ▶   Date ▶

Part 2—Tax Computation

1	Enter the amount from Schedule A, Part 3, line 15	1	
2	Enter the amount from Schedule B, line 3	2	
3	Total taxable gifts (add lines 1 and 2)	3	
4	Tax computed on amount on line 3 (see Table for Computing Tax in separate instructions). . .	4	
5	Tax computed on amount on line 2 (see Table for Computing Tax in separate instructions). . .	5	
6	Balance (subtract line 5 from line 4)	6	
7	Maximum unified credit (nonresident aliens, see instructions)	7	192,800 00
8	Enter the unified credit against tax allowable for all prior periods (from Sch. B, line 1, col. C) .	8	
9	Balance (subtract line 8 from line 7)	9	
10	Enter 20% (.20) of the amount allowed as a specific exemption for gifts made after September 8, 1976, and before January 1, 1977 (see instructions)	10	
11	Balance (subtract line 10 from line 9)	11	
12	Unified credit (enter the smaller of line 6 or line 11)	12	
13	Credit for foreign gift taxes (see instructions)	13	
14	Total credits (add lines 12 and 13)	14	
15	Balance (subtract line 14 from line 6) (do not enter less than zero)	15	
16	Generation-skipping transfer taxes (from Schedule C, Part 3, col. H, Total)	16	
17	Total tax (add lines 15 and 16)	17	
18	Gift and generation-skipping transfer taxes prepaid with extension of time to file . .	18	
19	If line 18 is less than line 17, enter BALANCE DUE (see instructions)	19	
20	If line 18 is greater than line 17, enter AMOUNT TO BE REFUNDED	20	

Under penalties of perjury, I declare that I have examined this return, including any accompanying schedules and statements, and to the best of my knowledge and belief it is true, correct, and complete. Declaration of preparer (other than donor) is based on all information of which preparer has any knowledge.

Donor's signature ▶   Date ▶

Preparer's signature (other than donor) ▶   Date ▶

Preparer's address (other than donor) ▶

Attach check or money order here.

For Paperwork Reduction Act Notice, see page 1 of the separate instructions for this form.   Cat. No. 16783M   Form **709** (Rev. 12-96)

Form **1041**
Department of the Treasury—Internal Revenue Service
U.S. Income Tax Return for Estates and Trusts

1996

For calendar year 1996 or fiscal year beginning _____ 1996, and ending _____ 19 ___

OMB No. 1545-0092

A Type of entity:
- ☐ Decedent's estate
- ☐ Simple trust
- ☐ Complex trust
- ☐ Grantor type trust
- ☐ Bankruptcy estate–Ch. 7
- ☐ Bankruptcy estate–Ch. 11
- ☐ Pooled income fund

B Number of Schedules K-1 attached (see instructions) ▶

Name of estate or trust (If a grantor type trust, see page 7 of the instructions.)

Name and title of fiduciary

Number, street, and room or suite no. (If a P.O. box, see page 7 of the instructions.)

City or town, state, and ZIP code

C Employer identification number

D Date entity created

E Nonexempt charitable and split-interest trusts, check applicable boxes (see page 8 of the instructions):
- ☐ Described in section 4947(a)(1)
- ☐ Not a private foundation
- ☐ Described in section 4947(a)(2)

F Check applicable boxes:
- ☐ Initial return
- ☐ Final return
- ☐ Amended return
- ☐ Change in fiduciary's name
- ☐ Change in fiduciary's address

G Pooled mortgage account (see page 9 of the instructions):
- ☐ Bought
- ☐ Sold
- Date:

Income

1	Interest income	1
2	Dividends	2
3	Business income or (loss) (attach Schedule C or C-EZ (Form 1040))	3
4	Capital gain or (loss) (attach Schedule D (Form 1041))	4
5	Rents, royalties, partnerships, other estates and trusts, etc. (attach Schedule E (Form 1040))	5
6	Farm income or (loss) (attach Schedule F (Form 1040))	6
7	Ordinary gain or (loss) (attach Form 4797)	7
8	Other income. List type and amount	8
9	**Total income.** Combine lines 1 through 8 ▶	9

Deductions

10	Interest. Check if Form 4952 is attached ▶ ☐	10
11	Taxes	11
12	Fiduciary fees	12
13	Charitable deduction (from Schedule A, line 7)	13
14	Attorney, accountant, and return preparer fees	14
15a	Other deductions NOT subject to the 2% floor (attach schedule)	15a
b	Allowable miscellaneous itemized deductions subject to the 2% floor	15b
16	**Total.** Add lines 10 through 15b	16
17	Adjusted total income or (loss). Subtract line 16 from line 9. Enter here and on Schedule B, line 1 ▶	17
18	Income distribution deduction (from Schedule B, line 17) (attach Schedules K-1 (Form 1041))	18
19	Estate tax deduction (including certain generation-skipping taxes) (attach computation)	19
20	Exemption	20
21	**Total deductions.** Add lines 18 through 20 ▶	21

Tax and Payments

22	Taxable income. Subtract line 21 from line 17. If a loss, see page 13 of the instructions	22
23	**Total tax** (from Schedule G, line 8)	23
24	**Payments: a** 1996 estimated tax payments and amount applied from 1995 return	24a
b	Estimated tax payments allocated to beneficiaries (from Form 1041-T)	24b
c	Subtract line 24b from line 24a	24c
d	Tax paid with extension of time to file: ☐ Form 2758 ☐ Form 8736 ☐ Form 8800	24d
e	Federal income tax withheld. If any is from Form(s) 1099, check ▶ ☐	24e
	Other payments: **f** Form 2439 _____ ; **g** Form 4136 _____ ; Total ▶	24h
25	**Total payments.** Add lines 24c through 24e, and 24h ▶	25
26	Estimated tax penalty (see page 13 of the instructions)	26
27	**Tax due.** If line 25 is smaller than the total of lines 23 and 26, enter amount owed	27
28	**Overpayment.** If line 25 is larger than the total of lines 23 and 26, enter amount overpaid	28
29	Amount of line 28 to be: **a** Credited to 1997 estimated tax ▶ _____ ; **b** Refunded ▶	29

Please Sign Here

Under penalties of perjury, I declare that I have examined this return, including accompanying schedules and statements, and to the best of my knowledge and belief, it is true, correct, and complete. Declaration of preparer (other than fiduciary) is based on all information of which preparer has any knowledge.

▶ _____ Signature of fiduciary or officer representing fiduciary — Date — EIN of fiduciary if a financial institution (see page 4 of the instructions)

Paid Preparer's Use Only

Preparer's signature ▶	Date	Check if self-employed ▶ ☐	Preparer's social security no.
Firm's name (or yours if self-employed) and address ▶		EIN ▶	
		ZIP code ▶	

For Paperwork Reduction Act Notice, see page 1 of the separate instructions.   Cat. No. 11370H   Form **1041** (1996)

12/9/96   Published by Tax Management Inc., a Subsidiary of The Bureau of National Affairs, Inc.   1041.1

1997 Income Tax Rate Schedule for use by Estates and Nongrantor Trusts

Taxable Income

Over	But Not Over	Pay	% on Excess	Of the Over Amount
0	1,600	0	15	0
1,600	3,800	240	28	1,600
3,800	5,800	856	31	3,800
5,800	7,900	1,476	36	5,800
7,900	--------	2,232	39.6	7,900

Example: Assume that the Wilson Family Trust has taxable income in 1997 of $8,000. The tax due on this amount would be computed as follows:

(1) Select the appropriate line from the table below reflecting the total amount of income from the trust. In this example, $8,000 is greater than $7,900, so the fifth line in the table below contains the appropriate tax rate for this level of income.

(2) $2,232.00   Base tax due

   + 39.60   ($8,000 - $7,900 = 100 X 39.6 %)
   _____

   $2,271.60   Total tax due for 1997

CHAPTER 8

Your Net Worth for Federal Estate Tax Purposes

Your Net Worth for Federal Estate Tax Purposes

Many middle income individuals summarily assume that they are not "rich" and do not need to be concerned with estate tax planning. This assumption is often based upon a failure to analyze existing assets and to evaluate the increasing value of these assets in an inflationary economy. It is also based upon a misunderstanding of how the estate tax value of an individual's assets may differ from the value of those assets while the person is alive. Regardless of the reason for assuming that planning for estate taxes is unnecessary, this assumption may prove costly.

The Need for Careful Analysis

The key to an effective estate plan is to identify one's assets and determine their value for estate tax purposes.

An essential part of any estate analysis is to determine whether an individual may have a potential estate tax liability. If he does, he may wish to consider a number of techniques which will permit him to accomplish his objectives and minimize potential estate tax liability. The key to any effective estate plan is to identify one's assets and to determine their value for estate tax purposes.

The checklists at the end of Chapter 1 may be of some assistance in undertaking this analysis. Common errors in conducting this analysis include failing to take inflation into account or overlooking assets which are not immediately spendable. This may be illustrated by the following case history.

CASE IN POINT

Sam Smith is a 55-year-old retired senior government executive and his wife, Susan, is a 53-year-old public school teacher. Sam started a successful consulting business following his retirement from the federal government. He earns $60,000 per year and Susan earns $30,000 from her employment. They own their home as tenants by the entirety. When the first spouse dies, they want everything to go to the surviving spouse so he or she can live in financial security. When the survivor dies, the want everything to be split between their two children. They want simple wills to accomplish their objectives. In their view their net worth is less than $600,000, and they think they do not need any tax planning. Sam recently inherited $150,000 from his mother's estate. They conclude that their assets are as follows:

Home	$300,000
Inheritance	150,000
Savings, Stocks, etc.	<u>50,000</u>
Total	$500,000

In making their analysis Sam and Susan used a 5-year-old property tax appraisal that understated the current value of their house by $100,000. They overlooked a $250,000 insurance policy on Sam's life, and they failed to include the value of their cars and miscellaneous personal effects worth approximately $30,000. They failed to include the approximately $50,000 that was in Susan's pension account.[5]

After professional consultation, it was finally determined that the total value of Sam and Susan's property is $930,000 and not the $500,000 they had estimated. It became apparent that Sam and Susan have a potential estate tax problem; however, this problem could be easily resolved by using a simple <u>bypass trust.</u> The trust also took into account that the Smiths' assets could appreciate substantially prior to their death without causing an added estate tax liability. The tax cost of Sam and Susan's failure to properly analyze their assets is as follows:

<u>Tax Result with Simple Wills</u>

	Tax Due
At death of 1st to die	-0-
At death of 2nd to die	$125,700
Net to children	
($930,000 - $125,700)	$804,300

<u>Tax Result with a Bypass Trust</u>

	Tax Due
At death of first spouse	-0-
At death of second spouse	-0-
Net to children	$930,000
Net saving	$125,700

[5] They also failed to include the value of any spousal survivor annuity which would be included in Sam's estate if he died first. The value of this survivor annuity would qualify for the marital deduction upon the death of the first spouse. Because the right to the annuity would terminate on the death of the survivor, it would have no effect on the amount of the estate tax payable.

Sam and Susan's assumption that they were not rich and did not need to do any estate tax planning could have resulted in a $125,700 error. Fortunately, this error was discovered and a plan was implemented to avoid it.

Estate Tax Valuation

The obvious first step in any estate tax plan is to determine what assets a person has and how they will be valued for federal estate tax purposes. In most instances the fair market value of an asset for estate tax purposes is easy to determine; however, special rules may apply to life insurance, survivor annuities, or pension benefits.

Life Insurance

A whole life or universal life policy have a cash surrender value. A term policy does not.

The fair market value of a life insurance policy during the life of the insured is the cash surrender value of the policy, if any. Typically a <u>whole life</u> or <u>universal life</u> policy will have a cash surrender value. A <u>term policy,</u> however, does not have a cash surrender value. It provides pure insurance in that it is only worth something upon the death of the insured. Thus, for purposes of determining an individual's net worth, an insurance policy will undoubtedly be worth substantially less than its face value. When the insured dies, the full value of the policy proceeds may be includable in the estate of the insured. (See Chapter 10 for a discussion of the various types of life insurance policies and the estate tax implications of owning insurance.)

CASE IN POINT

Peter McGuire is a 45-year-old male who purchased a term life insurance policy with a face value of $500,000. His current annual premium is $800 per year. The policy will remain in force as long as Peter continues to pay the annual premium. Because the policy is a term policy, it has no cash surrender value and its only value to Peter is the insurance protection it provides.

It is of no value in determining his net worth; however, if Peter were to die while the policy is in force, the full amount of the policy proceeds, $500,000, is includable in his gross estate. Thus, its value for purposes of planning Peter's estate is $500,000.

The Estate Tax Value of a Survivor Annuity

Many persons save for their retirement by purchasing an annuity either through a commercial insurance carrier or by participating in an annuity program sponsored by their employer. Under virtually all retirement plans sponsored by government employers, an annuity is either the required form of benefit or at least an optional form of benefit. This means that if an employee participates in the retirement program, he either must or may choose an annuity as the form of retirement benefit. The right to a survivor benefit is also quite common, and in certain instances may be required.

The right of an annuitant's survivor to continue to receive monthly payments has a value that must be determined for federal estate tax purposes. Determining the value of a commercial annuity is relatively straightforward. Its value is its replacement cost, or the amount it would cost to buy an annuity from a private company providing similar benefits.

Under government retirement plans, an annuity is either the required form of benefit or an optional one.

A survivor annuity paid to the spouse of a deceased government annuitant is not a commercial annuity. The value of such an annuity is the present value of the right to receive future payments.

The present value of a survivor annuity requires an analysis of a number of variable factors, including the age of the survivor, the monthly amount paid under the annuity at the time of death, the life expectancy of the survivor, and a variable rate of interest published by the Internal Revenue Service on a periodic basis.

103

Spousal Annuity and the Marital Deduction

If the person who qualifies for a survivor annuity is the spouse of the decedent, the value of the spousal annuity is fully includable in the gross estate of the decedent. This will not, however, result in an increase in the estate's tax liability because of the applicability of the marital deduction. (See Chapter 7 for a discussion of the marital deduction.)

CASE IN POINT

Jane and Lamar Kennedy, ages 52 and 68 respectively, were married for 20 years prior to Lamar's death in 1997. Lamar retired from the federal government in 1986 and at the time of his death he was receiving a monthly annuity of about $3,000. Following Lamar's death, Jane receives a survivor annuity of $1,650 per month. The present value of this survivor annuity was determined to be $200,000, and this amount was included in Lamar's gross estate for federal estate tax purposes.

Lamar's other assets were worth $420,000, and he left these assets to Jane in his will. Lamar's gross estate was $620,000. Accordingly, his estate was required to file a federal estate tax return; however, because all of his property was left to his wife, it qualified for the marital deduction and there was no estate tax liability.

Pension Plan Assets

Benefits to survivors from a qualified pension plan are includable in the decedent's gross estate.

Benefits payable to a decedent's survivors from a qualified pension plan are includable in the decedent's gross estate. The federal CSRS, FERS and the retirement plans of most state and local governments are treated as qualified plans. If the plan benefit is payable in a lump sum, the amount included in the gross estate is simply the amount of the lump sum. If the benefit is payable in the form of an annuity, its value is the present value determined in the manner described above.

Special Exclusion - Pre-1984 Retirees

Prior to 1982 any benefits payable from a qualified plan upon the death of a plan participant were excluded from the gross estate of the decedent. This favorable tax treatment was modified in 1982. In place of the unlimited exclusion, the excludable amount was limited to $100,000. In 1984 the $100,000 exclusion was repealed and the full value of a decedent's interest in a qualified plan became includable in the gross estate.

As part of both the 1982 and 1984 tax acts, certain distributions from a qualified plan continued to receive favored treatment under two transitional rules.

The first transitional rule provides that the entire amount of the annuity may be excluded from the gross estate if the decedent was in a pay status on December 31, 1982, and, prior to December 31, 1982, the decedent had irrevocably elected a survivor benefit.

Certain pre-1984 annuities may be wholly or partially excluded from estate tax.

The second transitional rule provides that the repeal of the $100,000 exclusion does not apply to the estates of any individuals who were in a pay status as of December 31, 1984, and who prior to July 18, 1984, irrevocably elected the form of benefit that their survivor would receive.

The term pay status as used in these transitional rules means that an individual is actually receiving retirement benefits. The irrevocable election refers to an election to provide a spousal annuity benefit which may not be changed. The election of any individual who elected a spousal annuity benefit prior to 1984 is irrevocable.

CASE IN POINT

Dick Duncan retired from his position with the federal government on May 15, 1984 at the age of 55. On June 15, 1984 he notified the Office of Personnel Management of his irrevocable election to provide a survivor annuity to his 30-year-old wife Diane. When Dick died in April, 1991, his personal representative determined that the value of the survivor annuity was $230,000.

Dick's estate may exclude $100,000 of this amount because he was receiving an annuity on December 31, 1984 and was therefore in a pay status. Moreover, he has made an irrevocable election before July 18, 1984 to provide these benefits to his spouse. If, prior to December 31, 1982, Dick had retired, started to receive annuity payments, and elected a survivor annuity, his estate would have been eligible to exclude the full amount of the survivor annuity.

Conclusion

The first step in any estate plan is to determine what assets a person has and how they will be valued for federal estate tax purposes. When this is done it is possible to develop an estate plan that accomplishes the person's goals while limiting tax liability.

CHAPTER 9

Practical Alternatives for Making Gifts to Children

Practical Alternatives for Making Gifts to Children

For many, the simplest and most practical transfer method of a small amount of property is an outright gift.

Parents, grandparents or other adults frequently wish to make gifts to minor and adult children. If the gift is large enough to cause a potential gift tax liability (i.e., more than $10,000) the person making the gift (the donor) may wish to establish a trust. (See Chapter 11 for the advantages of establishing a trust.) In some situations, however, a trust is simply not a practical option. For many middle income persons, the cost of creating and administering a trust is not practical. Individuals who wish to transfer a relatively small amount of property may find that the simplest and most practical transfer method is an outright gift. Small sums of money, heirlooms, or property that do not require management or investment supervision are generally best transferred outright.

What Makes a Gift Valid

There are three essential requirements the donor must satisfy for a gift to be valid. First, he must intend to make a gift. Second, the donor must deliver the property to the recipient. Third, the recipient of the property must accept the gift. It is especially important that persons who are making lifetime gifts to reduce their taxable estate ensure that these requirements are satisfied. Failure to do so may mean that the value of the gift property will be included in the donor's taxable estate.

CASE IN POINT

Stanley Bishop established a bank account in the name of William Bishop, his 12-year-old grandson. Stanley retained the right to withdraw funds from the account as long as he lived. He also retained the passbook which showed the amount of funds in his account. When Stanley died, there was $50,000 in the account. This full amount was includable in his gross estate. Since Stanley retained control over the account, no completed gift was made.

The disadvantage of any outright gift to a minor child is that it gives a child control over money or property which he may not be able to manage intelligently. Fortunately, a low cost practical alternative is available.

Gifts to Minors

The Uniform Gifts To Minors Act (UGMA) and Uniform Transfers to Minors Act (UTMA) permit the establishment of a custodial account. In such an account, the gifts to the minor are held by a custodian. The custodian may either simply hold the assets in an investment account or use them to pay college or other support and maintenance expenses of the child. UGMA or UTMA transfers are irrevocable, and except in cases of disability or incompetence, all assets in the account must be turned over to the minor when he/she reaches the age of majority.

Virtually all states have adopted the UGMA, the UTMA, or both. These laws permit money, real estate, limited partnership interests, patents, tangible personal property, and other forms of property to be transferred.

The UGMA and UTMA are accounts where the gifts to a minor are held by a custodian.

The transfer instrument, generally a simple, pre-printed form available through most financial institutions (such as banks, stock brokers, mutual fund companies, and savings and loans), must contain specific language to effect the transfer, i.e., "I, John Doe, hereby complete a gift to my daughter, Jane, a minor, pursuant to the Uniform Gifts to Minors Act as codified at Section 1.1 of the Corporate Code of this State."

The financial institution can advise customers of the proper language and provide all other necessary documentation to effect the transfer. The donor merely needs to provide the minor's social security number and then appoint a reliable person (usually a relative or the parent himself) as custodian and transfer the funds to the account. All of this can be accomplished in a matter of minutes. It is not necessary to pay a lawyer to establish the custodial account, and it is not necessary for the custodian to make any accounting or to file trust income tax returns.

There are some disadvantages to UGMA or UTMA gifts. They are irrevocable and all assets must be turned over to the child at the age of majority which may be considered by many a relatively young age. In some states, the custodian has narrow investment powers, and in others, restrictions are placed on the type of property that can be transferred.

UGMA or UTMA gifts offer a simple, hassle-free and inexpensive way to set aside funds for future use by a minor child without establishing a formal trust.

Further, any income on UGMA or UTMA property is taxable to the minor child. If the minor child has more than $650 of income in any one year, he is required to file a federal income tax return (and possibly a state income tax return as well) and pay appropriate income taxes. If the minor child is under 14 and has unearned (i.e., investment) income of more than $1,500 in any one year, this income is subject to federal income tax at his parents' tax rate. This is known as the kiddie tax. If the child has earned income, such as by working in his parents' store, he pays tax on the "earned" income at the applicable "earned" rate, not at his parents' rate.

When a child reaches 14, the kiddie tax is no longer applicable, and any income, either earned or unearned, is then taxed at the child's own rate, regardless of the amount. A parent, however, remains legally obligated to ensure that the child satisfies all tax obligations.

Although UGMA or UTMA gifts have disadvantages, by and large they offer a simple, hassle-free, and inexpensive way for individuals to set aside funds for future use by a minor child without establishing a formal trust.

Gifts to Adult Children

As explained in Chapter 7, an individual is entitled to claim an annual gift tax exclusion of $10,000 per donee (the gift recipient) per year and pay no gift tax. Thus, if a person makes gifts of $10,000 each to ten (10) separate individuals in any calendar year, he may give $100,000 in tax free gifts in that one year. The exclusion is available on an annual basis and a new exclusion is available each tax year. Therefore, if a person wishes to make total tax-free gifts of $100,000 to an adult child over a period of time, he may do so by giving $10,000 each year for 10 years.

In addition, the $10,000 annual exclusion can be increased to $20,000 if a married couple makes a split gift. The wife can give $20,000 to an individual, such as an adult daughter, and if her husband joins in making the split gift election, the daughter receives $20,000, but her parents pay no gift tax.

The couple must file a gift tax return in this instance to make the split gift election, on which they must indicate that they both consent to the split gift during the calendar year. (See discussion in Chapter 7.)

CASE IN POINT

Debra proposes to make a gift of two parcels of real property, each worth approximately $80,000, to each of her two adult children, Tom and Jeanne. If Debra transferred her entire ownership interest in one parcel to Tom, she would have made a gift of $80,000 to Tom.

After applying the $10,000 annual exclusion, the taxable gift to Tom is $70,000. If this transfer were the only taxable gift she had made, the tax on it would be $15,600. If she made identical gifts to both Tom and Jeanne in the same tax year, she would have made total taxable gifts of $140,000. The gift tax on the two gifts would be $35,800.

Debra may use several simple techniques to either minimize or avoid a gift tax liability. She may achieve her objective of giving the property to her children by transferring one-half of her interest in each parcel to her children as a joint tenant with a right of survivorship. The value of one-half of each parcel is $40,000. After applying the $10,000 annual exclusion, Debra has made a taxable gift to each of her children of $30,000. Assuming she makes only one gift during the year, the tax on a $30,000 gift (i.e., $40,000 - $10,000 annual exclusion) would be $6,000.

If she made two gifts of a one-half interest to each of her children, the total value of these gifts would be $80,000; the taxable gift would be $60,000, and the gift tax liability would be $13,000. Thus, by making gifts of a one-half interest, Debra accomplishes her objective of giving an interest in her property to her children.

Moreover, since these interests are in joint tenancy with the right of survivorship, they will not be subject to probate at Debra's death. By using this simple planning technique, she may realize tax savings of $22,800. (NOTE: By doing this, Debra's children would not be able to use the benefits of a stepped-up basis. See discussion in Chapter 7.)

The Unified Credit

The use of the unified credit may be illustrated by applying it to the example discussed earlier. Assuming the donor has not previously used her unified credit, this credit may be applied to offset the gift taxes which would otherwise be due. Thus, if Debra made both gifts of her entire interest in the property, she would report a gift tax liability of $35,800. By using the unified credit, she will be able to fully offset this liability and no tax will be due when the gift tax return is filed. After reducing the $192,800 credit by the amount claimed, the donor has a remaining credit of $157,000 (i.e., $192,800 - $35,800 = $157,000).

Tax Return Must Be Filed

A donor is required to file a gift tax return even if no gift tax is due.

Even though no gift tax may be due in the above example, the donor is nevertheless required to file a gift tax return. A gift tax return must be filed for all gifts except: 1) gifts to a spouse, or 2) gifts worth less than $10,000 and which are eligible for the annual gift tax exclusion. The gift tax return is an annual return and it must be filed between January 1 and April 15 of the year following the calendar year when the gifts were made.

If the donor in the above example made a gift of one parcel of property on December 30, 1996, and a gift of the second parcel of property on January 2, 1997, the return for the first gift would be due on or before April 15, 1997. The return for the second gift would be due on or before April 15, 1998.

Life Insurance

CHAPTER 10: Life Insurance

Life Insurance

When many persons think of life insurance, their first thought is of the unsolicited mail or telephone calls they receive from insurance agents. A typical reaction may be "my employer provides a $50,000 policy on my life and I don't need any more insurance." This may not always be a wise point of view.

Any estate or financial plan involves a consideration of the need for life insurance.

Any estate or financial plan involves a consideration of the need for life insurance. People usually buy life insurance for one of three reasons. The most common reason is to protect a person's family in the event of the early death of the principal wage earner. A second reason applies to individuals who have acquired substantial assets that might not be liquid (i.e., easy to sell quickly.) These assets could include valuable real estate, objects of art or business interests. For these individuals, life insurance provides a source of liquid funds which may be used to pay estate taxes or other estate settlement costs. A third reason for buying life insurance applies to business owners who may wish to use life insurance proceeds to buy out the interests of a deceased co-owner.

This discussion is limited to the individual who buys (or should buy) life insurance to protect his family in the event of an early death. If others depend upon an individual for support, that individual probably needs life insurance. The obvious question is how much life insurance is needed? Answering this question requires a consideration of the following:

• How much income will my family need if I die?

• What sources of income will my family have if I die?

• How much income will any insurance proceeds be able to produce?

Numerous other factors may be relevant in any given situation; however, consideration of these specific factors will provide some general guidance regarding the need for life insurance.

CASE IN POINT

George Kemp is a 35-year-old married federal employee who has two children. George's annual salary is $48,000 per year. His wife, Sharon, works part-time and earns about $8,000 per year. The Kemp family tries to save about $200 per month for their children's education and they are generally able to do this. Their major obligations include a $125,000 mortgage on their home and a $300 monthly car payment. George's only insurance coverage is a $100,000 policy provided under the FEGLI (Federal Employees Group Life Insurance) program.

If George dies before Sharon, she would need $48,000 in income to replace George's lost salary. While she believes she may be able to get a full-time job, she is concerned about how long this would take and how much she could earn. She is also afraid that if George were to die, she would be forced to sell their house. George may wish to make a conservative assumption that he needs to buy enough life insurance to replace his $48,000 annual income. If he assumes that the insurance proceeds can be reinvested at a rate of 8 percent per year, he will need $600,000 in insurance (i.e., $600,000 x .08 = $48,000) to reach his goal. Since George's employer provides a $100,000 policy, he needs $500,000 in additional insurance to provide the funds necessary to adequately protect his family. He should be able to but this amount of term insurance for about $500 per year.

Types of Insurance

There are many types of insurance, but three of the most common are whole life, term, and universal life. A typical whole life policy provides a specified amount of insurance (i.e., $500,000) for a level premium (i.e., $7,000 per year.) A whole life insurance policy provides both an investment and insurance. The investment builds in the form of a cash surrender value and is typically paid along with the insurance upon the death of the insured. Some plans permit the insured to terminate the whole life policy and cash it in for the cash surrender value which has accrued over the years. The cost of a $500,000 whole life policy for a healthy 35-year-old nonsmoking male would be approximately $7,000 per year.

A whole life insurance policy provides both an investment and insurance.

Assuming that the $7,000 premium were paid in full for six and one-half years, the cash surrender value would have accrued by the seventh year of the policy so that all future premiums could be fully paid by the accumulated cash dividends. In addition to an increasing cash surrender value, the amount of death benefit paid may also increase. Thus, in this example, by the time the insured reaches his 55th birthday, the policy could have a cash value of $145,000 and a death benefit of $645,000.

A term policy provides insurance only without any cash buildup while a universal life policy provides some cash buildup and the premium may change each year.

A term policy provides insurance only without any cash buildup. It provides a specific amount of insurance (i.e., $500,000) and the policy premium must be paid each year. The amount of the policy premium usually increases each year. Because there is no cash surrender value in the policy, a term policy is usually much cheaper than a whole life policy. The cost of a $500,000 term life insurance policy for a healthy 35-year-old nonsmoking male is approximately $510 per year, increasing to as much as $1,800 per year by the time the insured is 55-years-old.

A universal life policy is designed to combine the benefits of whole life and term life insurance. It provides some cash buildup and the premium may change each year. It is somewhat more expensive than the term policy because it provides both insurance and an investment. The cost of a $500,000 universal life insurance policy for a healthy 35-year-old nonsmoking male is approximately $2,500 per year and may build up as much as $75,000 cash value within the first 20 years.

The price for policies providing similar coverage may vary widely from company to company. The figures provided are those charged by one insurance company and are provided solely for illustrative purposes.

How to Select the Best Insurance

The obvious question for any purchaser of insurance is how to get the best coverage for the lowest cost. Such publications as *Consumer Reports* provide periodic comparisons of the coverage provided by insurance companies. Moreover, A.M. Best & Co., an insurance rating institution, rates insurance companies on a regular basis. It is usually advisable to buy insurance from a company rated A+ on the Best rating system. This provides some assurance of the financial solvency of the company. The A.M. Best & Co. rating information is generally available at most public libraries.

In addition, there are at least three organizations which will provide comparative quotes on term insurance comparisons. Insurance Information (800-472-5800) charges approximately $50 for its services (the service is free if they do not save you money.) Insurance Quotes (800-972-1104) and Select Quote (800-343-1985) do not charge a fee for their services.

Tax Considerations

A significant tax advantage of using life insurance is that the Internal Revenue Code specifically excludes life insurance proceeds from the taxable income of the recipient of these proceeds. Thus, there is no federal *income* tax liability on the receipt of life insurance proceeds. Life insurance proceeds may be subject, however, to the federal *estate* tax. The proceeds of any life insurance policy are included in the decedent's gross estate if he owns the policy at the time of his death or if the proceeds are payable to his estate.

The IRS excludes life insurance proceeds from the taxable income of the recipient of these proceeds.

While everyone may not need life insurance, it is something that everyone should consider. Most financial advisers or estate planners are knowledgeable about insurance and will be able to provide unbiased advice regarding the need for insurance.

CHAPTER 11

Using Trusts in Implementing Estate Planning Goals

Using Trusts in Implementing Estate Planning Goals

A trust is one of the tools available to assist an individual in achieving his estate planning goals. It may also be used to aid in managing assets during life, either as a supplement to or substitute for a will. While trusts may be viewed as a tool for wealthy persons with substantial estates, they may also provide significant benefits to persons of modest means. Revocable living trusts may be particularly useful for middle income individuals. Irrevocable trusts, however, are frequently used for tax planning purposes and may only be feasible for persons who have assets in excess of $600,000.

What is a Trust and How is it Structured?

Every trust has a grantor, trustee and at least one beneficiary.

A trust is an agreement in which one person, the trustee, holds and manages property transferred to the trust by the grantor for the benefit of another, the beneficiary. Every trust has a grantor, trustee and at least one beneficiary. In certain trusts, the same person may occupy all three positions. The grantor establishes the trust by entering a trust agreement with the trustee. The trust agreement describes the property transferred to the trust, names the trustees and beneficiaries, and outlines the scope of the trustee's authority. The trust agreement also describes when and under what conditions payments may be made to beneficiaries. The first and last pages of a sample revocable living trust appear at the end of this chapter.

The grantor (also sometimes referred to as the settlor) is the person who creates the trust and owns the asset(s) placed in trust. The grantor determines what property will be transferred to the trust, how this property will be managed, and when and under what circumstances it will be transferred to the beneficiary. The trust estate (sometimes referred to as the trust corpus) can be property the grantor presently possesses such as cash or property which will be paid to the trust in the future such as life insurance proceeds.

The trustee is obligated to act in the best interest of the beneficiary.

The trustee is the individual, or institution, responsible for managing the trust property for the benefit of the beneficiaries named in the trust. The trustee's powers and duties are specified in the trust agreement and the trustee must at all times act in accordance with the trust agreement. The trustee is obligated to act in the best interest of the beneficiary.

As the name implies, the beneficiary is the person or persons for whom the trust is created and who benefits from the trust. The trustee typically pays the beneficiary the income from the trust for a specified period of time before the trust terminates, at which time the remaining property is delivered to the beneficiary outright.

CASE IN POINT

Mike Smith enters into a trust agreement with XYZ Bank established for the benefit of his three children, Mary, Sue and Jim, ages 18, 20 and 22. Mike transfers $300,000 to XYZ Bank and instructs it to manage the property for the benefit of his children. Mary and Sue are presently in college and plan to attend graduate school. Jim is in his first year of medical school.

Under the trust agreement Mike directs the trustee to pay each of the children $10,000 in August of each year to assist in paying their educational expenses. When Mary, the youngest child, reaches age 25, the trustee is directed to distribute all funds remaining in the trust in equal one-third shares to his children.

In this situation, Mike is the grantor, XYZ Bank is the trustee and Mary, Sue and Jim are the beneficiaries. The funds transferred to the trust are the trust property or corpus. The trust will continue in existence until Mary reaches age 25. When all trust property is distributed, the trust will terminate.

Why Have a Trust?

Many individuals choose to transfer their assets through a trust because it is a private agreement. Unlike a will, a trust is not subject to probate and does not generally become a matter of public record. A properly drafted trust may enable a person to minimize attorneys' fees, court costs, and the delays frequently connected with probate proceedings. A trust may be created for the benefit of one or more persons and may frequently be used as part of a financial plan to limit tax liability. A significant advantage of a trust lies in its flexibility. It can do whatever the person establishing it wants it to do.

For example, a trust may be structured so that periodic distributions of income are made to one's survivors up to a specified age. Periodic distributions may also provide for the recipient's specified needs, such as payment of college expenses.

A trust can be a valuable tax planning tool and may be used to minimize income, estate or gift tax liability.

A trust can also protect the trust estate from claims of the recipients' creditors and can ensure that sufficient assets will exist to provide for the recipients' basic needs for the duration of the trust.

A trust can be a valuable tax planning tool and may be used to minimize income, estate or gift tax liability. If a trust is created to accomplish certain tax saving objectives, it should be reviewed any time there is a significant change in the tax laws.

CASE IN POINT

Thomas inherited $200,000 from his wealthy Aunt Becky when she died in February, 1980. On March 1, 1980, Thomas established a trust which will accumulate all trust income until his two sons, Ed and Bill, ages 12 and 14, reach college age. When they reach college age, all income will be distributed to them annually in August of each year to help pay their college expenses. The trust will terminate ten years and one day after it is established. At that time, the principal balance of $200,000 will be returned to Thomas.

Thomas created what is known as a <u>Clifford Trust.</u> A Clifford Trust is one which provides income to a beneficiary during the life of the trust. The trust terminates after a specified term of ten years or longer and all trust property is returned to the grantor.

Prior to the passage of the Tax Reform Act of 1986, a Clifford Trust was useful in permitting the grantor to avoid tax on the income generated by the trust without irrevocably giving up the trust property; however, the Tax Reform Act of 1986 changed the tax treatment of a Clifford Trust. As a result of this change, any income from a trust is taxable to the grantor if the trust property can revert to him. Obviously, this change in the tax law could have a sig-

A trust should be reviewed anytime there is a significan change in the tax laws.

nificant impact on Thomas's tax liability. Thus, after the passage of the Tax Reform Act of 1986, it would have been advisable for Thomas to consult with his attorney to determine whether anything could be done to minimize the impact of the tax changes on his estate planning goals.

Different Types of Trusts

If the grantor reserves the right to change the terms of the trust agreement during his lifetime, the trust is <u>revocable.</u> If he surrenders all rights to alter or amend the trust, it is <u>irrevocable.</u> A trust that is created and takes effect while the grantor is alive is a <u>living trust.</u> If the trust is created in the grantor's will or otherwise only takes effect at death, it is a <u>testamentary trust.</u>

Selecting a Trustee

A grantor may appoint as trustee himself, a family member, a trusted friend, a professional, such as an accountant, attorney or investment adviser, or an institution such as a bank or trust company. The trustee agrees to manage the trust property and to handle all administrative matters, such as investing trust proceeds and filing appropriate tax returns.

Some trusts are created specifically to obtain the benefit of professional management, such as in cases where a grantor is unable to locate a suitable trustee among his group of friends and relatives. In this situation, the trust agreement should specify the compensation to be paid the trustee. Any institutional trustee will require that the amount of fees it will receive for serving as trustee must be specified in the trust agreement.

Consult with several banks or trust companies before selecting an institutional trustee.

There is a wide variance in both fees charged by institutional trustees and the minimum amount of assets an institutional trustee will require to be in the trust before agreeing to serve as trustee. For example, in the Washington, D.C. metropolitan area, the minimum amount a bank or trust company will accept for management may be as low as $50,000 or as high as $250,000. Similarly, the fees charged may range from less than 1 percent to more than 5 percent of the assets under management. Because of these variations, it is impossible to provide any guidelines of general applicability. It is advisable to consult several banks or trust companies before selecting an institutional trustee.

Before naming a trustee, the grantor must carefully weigh the reasons for selecting a trustee. In those cases where family members or trusted friends serve as trustee, the trustee may serve voluntarily and not require compensation from trust assets, resulting in a financial savings to the trust. In addition, a family member or trusted friend may be better than a professional trustee to discern the intent of the grantor in discretionary circumstances. In certain situations, it may be desirable to have co-trustees. One may be an institution or professional adviser who is experienced in managing investments and the other may be a friend or relative of the grantor who understands and respects his wishes. Regardless of whether one ultimately selects an individual or institution to serve as trustee, the grantor should make the selection only after having carefully considered the many options available to him and his goals for establishing the trust.

Limitations on Trust Uses

Trusts are popular estate planning tools because of their flexibility. Trusts can be created for any legal purpose; however, the law in virtually every state does limit the time that a trust can exist.

The <u>rule against perpetuities</u> is recognized in this country. It traces its origins to principles followed in England for several centuries. Its terms are so complex that even many skilled attorneys find its application baffling. Its purpose is to prevent a grantor from indefinitely limiting the transfer of property. It provides that title to property left in a trust must transfer to the ultimate recipient within a specified period

The law in virtually every state does limit the time that a trust can exist.

after the grantor's death. For example, Price is a wealthy man who wishes to establish a trust for the purpose of providing college expenses for his grandchildren and all future generations of children born to his offspring. The provisions for the future generations would be illegal because the terms would be operative at an unreasonably remote and uncertain time in the future. These provisions would violate the rule against perpetuities.

(FIRST PAGE OF REVOCABLE LIVING TRUST)

EDWARD ROBERTS REVOCABLE LIVING TRUST

TRUST AGREEMENT made this _____day of _____,1994, between EDWARD ROBERTS of Washington, D.C., (hereinafter called the {Grantor") and EDWARD ROBERTS (hereinafter called the "Trustee.")

1. Trust Property. The name of the Trust shall be "the EDWARD ROBERTS REVOCABLE LIVING TRUST" ("the Revocable Trust"). The Grantor hereby transfers and delivers to the Trustee the property listed in the annexed Schedule A ("the Trust Property"), to have and to hold, the receipt of which is acknowledged by the Trustee, and any other property which the Grantor may transfer at any time to the Trustee for the uses and purposes and upon the terms and conditions herein set forth.

2. Beneficiaries. The primary beneficiary of the EDWARD ROBERTS REVOCABLE TRUST shall be EDWARD ROBERTS during his lifetime. Upon the death of EDWARD ROBERTS, the Successor Beneficiary of the EDWARD ROBERTS REVOCABLE TRUST shall be WILLIAM THOMAS of Greensboro, North Carolina.

3. Trustees. During the lifetime of Grantor, the Trustee of the EDWARD ROBERTS REVOCABLE LIVING TRUST shall be EDWARD ROBERTS. Upon the death or incapacity of EDWARD ROBERTS, WILLIAM THOMAS of Greensboro, North Carolina. shall serve as Successor Trustee. If WILLIAM THOMAS is unable or unwilling to serve as Successor Trustee, ANNA REGER of Greensboro, N.C.

(LAST PAGE OF REVOCABLE LIVING TRUST)

10. <u>Governing Law.</u> This agreement and the trusts created by it have been accepted by the Trustee in the District of Columbia. All questions pertaining to the validity and construction of the agreement shall be determined, and the Trust shall be administered, under the law of the District of Columbia.

11. <u>Binding Agreement.</u> This agreement is binding and inures to the benefit of the parties and their respective executors, personal representatives, successors in interest and successors in trust.

IN WITNESS THEREOF, the parties hereto have signed this Agreement the day and year first above written.

_____
EDWARD ROBERTS, GRANTOR

_____
EDWARD ROBERTS, TRUSTEE

WITNESSES:
Printed_____Street_____
Signature_____City_____
Printed_____Street_____
Signature_____City_____
City of Washington
District of Columbia

Subscribed, sworn and acknowledged before me by EDWARD ROBERTS, _____and _____ this _____ day of _____, 1994.

_____
NOTARY PUBLIC

My commission expires:

CHAPTER 12

Revocable Living Trusts

Revocable Living Trusts

A <u>revocable living trust</u> is one that allows the grantor to transfer assets to a trust while he is alive and to change the terms of the trust at any time. It permits the grantor to retain control of his assets and is frequently suggested as a substitute for a will.[6] A revocable living trust does not offer any income or estate tax savings.

Advantages of a Revocable Living Trust

Perhaps the most significant advantage of any revocable trust is its flexibility. It permits the grantor to retain full control of all of his assets during his lifetime. If the trust is not working as the grantor planned, it may be changed or terminated.

A revocable trust is flexible and permits the grantor to retain full control of all of his assets during his lifetime.

A revocable living trust is a separate legal entity. It may be structured either to terminate at the grantor's death or to continue in existence after his death. A trust which is designed to avoid probate generally names the grantor as initial trustee and appoints a successor trustee. The successor may assume the role of trustee either when the original trustee becomes incompetent or when he dies. When the grantor dies, the successor is directed to distribute the assets in accordance with the grantor's wishes as expressed in the trust. A revocable living trust may also become irrevocable at the grantor's death.

If all of a grantor's property is held in a revocable trust, the trust is the legal owner of the property and this property is not subject to probate. If the trust works effectively, it is possible to minimize or avoid probate, with all of its attendant costs and delays.

---

[6]Numerous books have been written which suggest the use of a revocable trust as a tool to be used to avoid probate. Many times these books offer "do it yourself" kits for establishing your own revocable living trust.

CASE IN POINT

Richard Heller, an unmarried man of 52, establishes a revocable living trust and transfers all of his property to it. He is the grantor, trustee and beneficiary. The trust property will be managed for his benefit during his life. He names his only sister, Kathleen, as successor trustee. She will assume the role of trustee in the event of his death or incompetence.

When Richard dies, all of his property will be distributed in equal shares to Kathleen's two children. The trust also provides that if Kathleen's children are under the age of 25 at the time of his death, the successor trustee will continue to hold all property in trust until the youngest reaches age 25. She will then distribute the trust property in equal shares to the beneficiaries.

While the trust is revocable during Richard's life, it becomes irrevocable at his death. If everything Richard owns has been transferred to the trust at the time of his death, none of this property is subject to probate. If some, but not all, of Richard's property has been transferred to trust, only the property held in Richard's name is subject to probate.

Professional Management

A revocable living trust may also enable the grantor to obtain professional management of his assets by a bank, trust company, or other organization designed to provide investment advice. Most professional trustees require a certain minimum amount of the assets to be placed in trust before agreeing to serve as trustee. For example, in the Washington, D.C., metropolitan area, many banks and trust companies require a minimum of $250,000 in trust assets before undertaking the management of a trust. Other companies, however, will accept this responsibility if a minimum of $50,000 is placed in trust.

> **Most professional trustees require a certain minimum amount of the assets to be placed in trust before agreeing to serve as a trustee.**

Disadvantages of a Revocable Living Trust

Because of the complexity, fees for drafting a trust are generally higher than for the preparation of a will.

The creation of a trust may be more expensive than the preparation of a will because of the complexity of the instrument. Thus, fees for drafting the trust are generally higher than for the preparation of a will. Costs for simple wills and trusts vary, but in areas where a simple will may cost $300 to $500, a simple trust can cost as much as $1,000 to $1,500.

The trustee of many revocable living trusts is the grantor. If, however, a person other than the grantor serves as trustee, the trustee may require the trust to pay trustees' fees both at the time the trust is established and during the existence of the trust. The annual fee is generally stated as an annual percentage of assets under management (i.e., 3 percent of the first $100,000 and 1 percent of any assets in excess of $100,000.)

Since a trust is a separate legal entity, it is necessary to transfer legal ownership of trust property to the trust. If real estate is transferred to the trust, the deed to the property must be transferred from the name of the grantor to the name of the trust. This may (but generally does not) require the payment of local transfer taxes or other fees. If property held in a brokerage or bank account is part of the trust property, these accounts must be held in the name of the trust.

Generally, any income from a revocable trust is reported on the grantor's individual tax return under his social security number. While certain revocable trusts may require the trust to obtain a taxpayer identification number, this is generally not necessary. In certain limited circumstances, a revocable trust is a separate taxable entity and it may be treated as a separate taxpayer. If the grantor establishes a revocable living trust, retains the power to change it, but provides that the trust property can never revert to him, the trust may be treated as a separate taxable entity.

CASE IN POINT

Herb and Peggy Hill are both in their early 50s and they have two adult children. They own a home worth $150,000, have a bank account worth $20,000 and a mutual fund account worth $25,000. They decide to create the Hill Family Revocable Living Trust in order to avoid probate. They are co-grantors, co-trustees and co-beneficiaries of the trust. When they die, their son Louis will become successor trustee, sell all trust assets and divide the property in two equal shares and distribute this property to Louis and his sister Laura.

To accomplish these objectives, Herb and Peggy must transfer title of their home to the trust. This will require them to register a new deed listing the trust as owner of the property. The cost for preparation of the new deed may be as little as $150. Some states may require a transfer or recordation tax to be paid when the new deed is filed. The amount of this tax, when applicable, is usually from 1 to 3 percent of the value of the property. If a transfer tax applies, this could add from $1,500 to $4,500 to the cost of transferring the home to the trust. Ownership of Herb and Peggy's bank account and mutual fund account may be transferred through a representative of the bank or mutual fund company by completing the appropriate form.

Since Herb and Peggy are the grantors, trustees and beneficiaries of the Hill Family Revocable Living Trust, they do not need to apply for a separate tax identification number. They should continue to report all trust income on their federal tax return.

The disadvantages of a revocable living trust must always be weighed against the probate process.

The disadvantages of a revocable living trust must always be weighed against the probate process. Remember, if an individual holds property in his own name, it is subject to probate. If the decedent has a will, the executor files the will with the probate court. If the decedent dies without a will, it is necessary to petition the probate court to appoint an administrator, who is then responsible for distributing the decedent's property in accordance with state law.

Since probate proceedings are matters of public record, a will is open to public inspection. The probate process may also entail certain costs, such as executor's fees and attorneys' fees. Since the probate process is under the supervision of a court, certain delays that accompany the filing of any action in court are inevitable.

The creation of a revocable living trust permits the avoidance of the delays, costs and potential publicity often associated with probate.

CHAPTER 13

Irrevocable Trusts

Irrevocable Trusts

Irrevocable trusts are often used to assist in reducing tax liability. To achieve the desired tax benefits, it may be necessary for the grantor to relinquish any right to either manage the trust property or to use the income produced by the trust property. The grantor of an irrevocable trust must surrender his right to exercise any control whatsoever over the trust property if he wishes to have the property excluded from his gross estate.

The grantor of an irrevocable trust must surrender his right to exercise any control over the trust property.

As the name implies, the trust may not be revoked after it has been created. The major advantage to be gained by surrendering the right to control trust property is the ability of the grantor to reduce significantly both income and estate tax liability. If the grantor wishes to realize these tax benefits, however, he cannot be either the trustee or the beneficiary of the trust. Thus, an irrevocable trust should be used only when the grantor has assets he is certain he will not need during his lifetime.

Income Tax Considerations

An irrevocable trust is a separate legal and taxable entity. It must obtain a separate taxpayer identification number, and it is required to file an annual income tax return on IRS Form 1041. It accounts for its income and deductions on this return in a manner similar to that of an individual taxpayer. A grantor seeking to reduce income tax liability may transfer either income-producing assets or assets which have substantially appreciated to the trust. Once the property is transferred to the trust, the grantor is no longer liable for any tax attributable to income from the property.

The trust is entitled to a deduction for any amounts distributed to trust beneficiaries. A beneficiary who receives a distribution of trust income is subject to income tax on the distribution. Thus, an irrevocable trust can produce significant overall income tax savings if the trust, the beneficiary, or both are in a lower tax bracket than the grantor. Finally, if property is held in trust and the grantor has surrendered all rights of ownership, the property is not subject to the federal estate tax at the time of the grantor's death.

CASE IN POINT

Pete Randolph is a retired government employee who has started a successful consulting firm. His annual annuity is $35,000 and he earns approximately $75,000 per year on a consulting contract with the National Institutes of Health. He is in the 36 percent federal income tax bracket. Pete transfers $100,000 to an irrevocable trust managed by an astute investment adviser. The trust will accumulate all income until the beneficiaries, his five children, reach age 21. Pete anticipates that the trust will earn at least $10,000 per year.

The income produced by the money transferred to the trust will be subject to income tax whether Pete retains these assets in his own name or transfers them to trust. If Pete retains these assets in his own name and they generate $10,000 in taxable income, he will owe a federal income tax of $3,600 on the investment proceeds.

If they are transferred to a trust and also generate $10,000 in taxable income in 1997, the income tax will be $3,039 because the trust is a separate taxable entity and is in a lower tax bracket than Pete.

Irrevocable trusts ensure that property passing to the beneficiaries has little or no estate tax liability.

Thus, $561 in federal income taxes will be saved by transferring these assets to the trust. Since Pete has irrevocably transferred these assets, they will not be subject to federal estate tax at the time of his death.

Estate Planning Uses

Irrevocable trusts are frequently used as part of an estate or financial plan. These trusts permit the grantor to ensure that his property passes to his intended beneficiaries and, with proper planning, to reduce or eliminate estate tax liability. Moreover, as is the case with revocable trusts, any property held in trust is not subject to the costs and delays frequently associated with the probate process.

CASE IN POINT

Fred Phelps, an 82-year-old widower, creates an irrevocable trust for the benefit of his three grandchildren, ages 6, 8 and 11. He initially transfers $30,000 to the trust and plans to contribute an additional $30,000 each year. The trust provides that all trust property will be accumulated until the youngest child reaches age 25. It will then be divided into three equal shares and distributed to the grandchildren.

Since the trust is irrevocable, Fred may not take any of the funds out of the trust even if he later needs these funds or if he learns that one of his grandchildren is an irresponsible spendthrift. None of the funds in the trust will be subject to the federal estate tax since Fred can transfer $10,000 to each grandchild annually free of tax. (See Chapter 7 and pages 148 and 149 for a discussion of the estate tax consequences of these transactions.)

Irrevocable Trust Considerations

An irrevocable trust is a valuable tool in planning an estate, but it should not be used without detailed advance planning. It is advisable for a person considering the establishment of such a trust to consider all of the implications of his action. While the tax savings may be substantial, the "price" paid for these benefits may also be substantial.

While tax savings may be substantial, the "price" paid for these benefits may also be substantial.

The tax and other planning considerations involved in the establishment of an irrevocable trust are quite complex and should only be undertaken by a person knowledgeable in these matters. Failure to properly implement an irrevocable trust could result in the worst possible situation: the irrevocable restriction of the grantor's right to use trust property without obtaining the desired tax benefits.

CHAPTER 14

Life Insurance Trusts

Life Insurance Trusts

A life insurance trust is a tool that permits a grantor to realize the tax savings of an irrevocable trust without having to part with substantial assets. If a grantor wishes to achieve significant estate tax savings without surrendering property he may need during his life, an irrevocable life insurance trust may be the answer. The primary purpose of purchasing life insurance is to provide funds to named beneficiaries upon the death of the insured grantor. Since these funds are only payable upon the death of the insured, they are obviously not available to him during his life.

Life insurance policies can play a vital role in devising an estate plan.

In a typical life insurance trust, the grantor either transfers an existing insurance policy to the trust or buys a new policy and names the trust the owner and beneficiary of the property. Transfer of ownership of an existing life insurance policy merely requires the completion of a change of ownership form with the insurer. A person should contact his insurance company with any questions about how to handle this procedure. All insurance companies are familiar with this procedure and will work with interested parties to assist them in accomplishing their objectives.

Certain policies, such as group insurance plans administered by federal or state governments, may not be eligible for transfer of ownership. The Office of Personnel Management has recently issued regulations that allow an insured federal employee or retiree to assign ownership of a FEGLI (Federal Employees Group Life Insurance) Policy to another individual or a trust. You may wish to discuss this with your employer if you have any questions about whether you may transfer ownership of a group term life insurance policy. Virtually all policies permit the owner to name the trust as beneficiary of the life insurance proceeds.

Life insurance proceeds can play a vital role in devising an estate plan. Because the Internal Revenue Code specifically excludes life insurance proceeds from the taxable income of the recipient, no federal income tax is imposed on either an individual or a trust upon the receipt of insurance proceeds. In most instances, absent a life insurance trust, life insurance proceeds are included in the gross estate of the insured for purposes of determining the amount of estate taxes which must be paid.

If the insured wishes to have the proceeds of a policy excluded from any estate tax liability, he must not retain ownership of the policy. If he does retain ownership, all proceeds of the policy will be includable in his gross estate. Absent transfer of ownership, this trust will have no significant estate tax advantages, but it will permit the owner of the policy to control the trust beneficiary's use of the life insurance proceeds. The named beneficiaries of an insurance policy will receive all proceeds regardless of whether the policy is transferred to a trust.

The grantor may fund a life insurance trust in a number of ways. He may make an initial payment to the trustee for the purpose of purchasing an insurance policy on the grantor's life. He may also contribute sufficient funds to pay future insurance premiums. Alternatively, he may make periodic contributions to the trust to pay future premiums. The trust is named as the owner of the life insurance policy. Since the insured has surrendered ownership in the policy, a properly drafted trust ensures that the policy proceeds will not be subject to the federal estate tax. A person whose net worth is $600,000 or more (including insurance) may wish to consider the use of a life insurance trust.

> **A life insurance trust has the tax planning benefit of an irrevocable trust without requiring the grantor to surrender an asset presently of use to him.**

Such a trust provides the major tax planning benefit of an irrevocable trust without having the major drawback of requiring the grantor to surrender an asset presently of use to him.

CASE IN POINT

Mike Richards is a 35-year-old married man with two children. He purchases a $500,000 life insurance policy and names his wife, Pat, as the sole beneficiary. The total value of Mike and Pat's other assets is approximately $150,000. Mike considers establishing a life insurance trust in order to avoid estate tax.

The $500,000 in insurance proceeds will be paid to Pat regardless of whether the policy is transferred to a life insurance trust. Unless the grantor specifically instructs the trustee, transfer of a policy to a trust will change the owner of the policy, not the beneficiary.

In Mike's situation, it is probably not advisable to use a life insurance trust. His reason for having life insurance is to protect his family in the event of his death, not to save taxes. Since all proceeds will be paid to Pat, they will qualify for the estate tax marital deduction and there will be no federal estate tax liability upon Mike's death. If his financial situation changes significantly in the future, he may wish to consider the advisability of establishing a trust at that time.

Funded and Unfunded Life Insurance Trusts

A funded trust is funded by income-producing assets while an unfunded trust has as its sole asset a life insurance policy or policies on the grantor's life.

There are two basic types of irrevocable life insurance trusts — funded and unfunded. A funded trust is typically funded with income-producing assets, such as dividend-producing stocks and bonds, in addition to one or more life insurance policies. A portion of the income generated by the trust is used to pay premiums on the life insurance policy.

In contrast, an unfunded trust has as its sole asset a life insurance policy or policies on the grantor's life. No income-producing property is available to provide funds to pay the premiums. As such, in order for the trustee to pay the premiums, the grantor must make periodic gifts to the trust for this purpose. There is a difference in the estate and gift tax results stemming from both types of trusts.

Tax Implications

An unfunded irrevocable life insurance trust relies upon gifts from the grantor to provide the funds needed to pay the life insurance premiums. Unless the trust is carefully structured, these gifts may be subject to federal gift tax.

The Internal Revenue Code authorizes an annual gift tax exclusion of up to $10,000 per donee per year for gifts of a present interest. A gift is of a present interest only if the recipient has the unrestricted right to the immediate use or benefit of the property transferred. The exclusion can be doubled to $20,000 if the donor is married and the spouse consents to the gift by making a split gift election. Gifts of a future interest, however, do not qualify for the annual exclusion since gifts of a future interest convey no immediate rights. (See Chapter 7 for discussion of gift tax implications.)

CASE IN POINT

Jenny establishes a life insurance trust for the benefit of her two children, Carson and Parker. She buys a $200,000 life insurance policy and transfers it to the trust. She agrees to contribute $2,000 annually to the trust to pay the premiums. Her $2,000 annual contribution to the trust is a gift. If her daughters have an immediate right to these funds, her annual contribution will be considered a present interest and will qualify for the annual gift tax exclusion of up to $10,000 per donee.

If they have no right to withdraw, it is a gift of a future interest because they can only benefit from this gift at some future time. If the daughters do not have a right to withdraw the annual premium payments, Jenny's gift will be considered a gift of a future interest and will be a taxable gift of $2,000. Thus, she must file a gift tax return and pay any applicable gift tax on the $2,000 gift. If Jenny has not used the full amount of her unified credit, no tax will be payable.

The Crummey Power How to Avoid Gift Tax[7]

If the grantor pays the premium directly to the insurance company, or if a cash gift is made to the trustee who immediately pays the premium, the gift will be treated as a gift of a future interest. This payment would be treated as a taxable gift for federal gift tax purposes and may cause a gift tax liability.[7]

A solution to this problem is to include a Crummey power in the trust.[8] Crummey powers are non-cumulative withdrawal rights of trust beneficiaries.

---

[7] See Chapter 7 for a discussion of gift tax consequences.
[8] The taxpayer who first used this type of provision and prevailed in a challenge by the IRS was Mr. Crummey.

Using this method, the grantor makes a gift of cash to be used for the payment of insurance premiums to the trust. In order for the gift to be a gift of a present interest and qualify for the $10,000 annual gift tax exclusion, the trust beneficiary must have the right to withdraw the gift from the trust, at least for a short period of time. The Crummey power allows the beneficiary to do this. If the beneficiary fails to exercise the withdrawal right, the power lapses and the trustee may then use the money to pay the life insurance premiums. Each beneficiary has a right to demand a distribution of any contribution for a specified period of time, typically 30 days.

There can be no advance agreement or understanding to limit a beneficiary's right to withdraw the gift despite the grantor's wishes.

Once a Crummey power is granted to a beneficiary of an irrevocable trust, the power to withdraw the gift may be exercised by the beneficiary despite the wishes of the grantor. It is generally expected and hoped that the beneficiary will not exercise the withdrawal power, but there can be no advance agreement or understanding to limit a beneficiary's right to avail himself of this privilege.

The grantor may provide in the trust agreement that contributions to the trust will be subject to the Crummey powers unless the grantor, at the time of the gift, specifies that the particular contribution may not be withdrawn. Should a beneficiary elect to exercise his withdrawal right, the grantor may specify that future contributions may not be withdrawn. This action will cause any future gift that cannot be withdrawn to fail to qualify for the gift tax annual exclusion.

CASE IN POINT

Mary Johnson is a 48-year-old widow who is employed as an engineer. She owns a $500,000 life insurance policy and the yearly premiums are $1,500.

She has named her two children, Jack and Alice, aged 22 and 25, respectively, as beneficiaries. She needs the protection provided by the insurance policy, but would like to avoid any estate tax liability. She would also like to have professional management of these funds if she dies before her children reach age 30.

Mary establishes an insurance trust for the benefit of her children with the XYZ Bank as trustee. Under the trust agreement, Mary agrees to transfer $2,000 or such greater amount as may be necessary from her personal bank account to pay the insurance premiums. The trust includes a Crummey power which gives each of the children a right to withdraw one-half of any amounts transferred to the trust within 30 days of receiving notice of this transfer. The trustee agrees to notify Jack and Alice in writing of any transfer to the trust. If Jack and Alice do not elect to withdraw this amount within 30 days, this right lapses and all funds are used to pay the policy premium. If Jack or Alice exercise this right, the trustee has the discretion to terminate the power to withdraw any future contributions made to the trust by Mary.

It is obviously contemplated that the children will not exercise the withdrawal right. If they do, it will be necessary for Mary to modify the methods to achieve her objectives. For example, she may stop making future payments to the trust. If she does, the trust will be unable to continue the life insurance coverage and the policy will lapse. Alternatively, the trustee may terminate the children's right to withdraw future contributions. If this happens, a gift tax may arise each time Mary makes a contribution to the trust. If Mary had not used her unified credit, no tax may be payable. To the extent a portion of this credit is used, it will not be available to offset any estate tax liability that may be payable upon her death.

CHAPTER 15

Miscellaneous Types of Trusts

Miscellaneous Types of Trusts

Certain trusts may be useful for persons regardless of their financial status.

Trusts can be used for many purposes. One of their primary advantages is the flexibility they afford to achieve the grantor's wishes.

There are a number of special-use trusts frequently used as part of an estate plan which require brief mention. Certain of these trusts, such as the standby trust or a pour-over trust, may be useful for persons regardless of their financial status. The other types of trusts discussed in this chapter, however, are used primarily to minimize taxes and are most often used by persons whose net worth exceeds $600,000.

Standby Trust

A <u>standby trust</u> is one which stands in readiness to take over and manage trust assets when the grantor is no longer able to manage them himself. It may provide for a takeover when the grantor is either mentally or physically unable to manage his affairs. It is not designed to save taxes, but it may be structured to do so. Its best use is generally to help an ailing individual overcome cumbersome and expensive incompetency proceedings under state law. These types of trusts are usually revocable, but need not be.

CASE IN POINT

Frances recently celebrated her 75th birthday. Her health is failing and she is concerned that she may not be able to continue to manage her affairs indefinitely. She drafts a standby trust which states that in the event she becomes incapacitated or unable to competently manage her affairs, her trust will be activated and her only child, Shirley, will serve as trustee.

Shirley will manage all trust assets for Frances's benefit until her death or until such time as the incapacity is removed. Upon Frances's death, Shirley will terminate the trust and will distribute all trust assets to herself. The trust should also include a provision specifying who will determine when Frances is no longer competent to manage her affairs. Typically, this determination is made either by a close friend, relative, or by one or more physicians.

Minor's Trust or Section 2503(c) Trust

A Section 2503(c) trust is one established for the benefit of a minor. It derives its name from the section of the Internal Revenue Code which authorizes it. Section 2503(c) is designed to permit a grantor to make a gift of a future interest to a trust established for the benefit of a minor without incurring any gift tax liability. As explained in Chapter 7, a gift only qualifies for the $10,000 annual gift tax exclusion if it is a gift of a present interest. Thus, unless the beneficiary of a trust has an immediate right of access to any property contributed to the trust, the gift will be considered to be a gift of a future interest and thus ineligible for the $10,000 annual gift tax exclusion.

Through a minor's trust, the grantor may keep trust income and principal out of the beneficiary's hands until he reaches age 21.

Section 2503(c) recognizes that while it may be desirable to make gifts to a trust for a minor, it is not desirable to give a minor child the immediate right of access to a large sum of money. It provides an exception to permit a gift of future interest to qualify for the gift tax exclusion. In a Section 2503(c) trust, the grantor gives up control of the trust property and the power to change the trust agreement. The grantor may keep trust income and principal out of the beneficiary's hands until he or she reaches age 21.

The trust can last even longer if it includes a Crummey power and the trust assets are not demanded by the beneficiary within 30 days after his or her 21st birthday.

CASE IN POINT

Mike and Mary Phillips contribute $10,000 per year to a trust for the benefit of their son, Tim, aged 8. The trust will accumulate all income and when Tim reaches age 21 he may withdraw all funds then in the trust. If Tim does not notify the trustee that he wishes to withdraw these funds within 30 days of his 21st birthday, his right of withdrawal lapses. The trustee will then retain all funds in trust for Tim's benefit. He will pay Tim $10,000 annually on his birthday. When Tim reaches his 30th birthday, all funds remaining in trust will be paid to him and the trust will terminate.

The trust is a Section 2503 (c) trust. Although Tim has no immediate right of access to the property, the $10,000 annual gift qualifies for the annual gift tax exclusion. Tim has a right of access to all trust property when he reaches age 21. The provision in the trust which states that if he does not exercise this right of access within 30 days of reaching his 21st birthday is the Crummey Power.

Pour-Over Trust

A pour-over trust may be either revocable or irrevocable.

The pour-over trust is a trust in which assets are poured over into the trust from another source. The trust is the recipient of the poured over assets. The pour-over may be from the grantor's will or from another source outside the estate such as insurance proceeds. Such a trust may be either revocable or irrevocable.

CASE IN POINT

Liza has an estate valued at $1.2 million. She wishes to leave her entire estate to her church and several charities which she has generously supported throughout her lifetime as an anonymous donor. Knowing that her will is subject to public inspection, Liza drafts a will stating that after all of her taxes and other valid claims against her estate have been satisfied, her remaining assets will be paid to the trustee of the private trust she has established. In the trust, Liza designates her church and the charities as beneficiaries.

Although public inspection of Liza's will would reveal that she had left her assets to a trust, the particulars of the trust including the identity of the beneficiaries and the manner in which the assets are distributed will not be revealed.

Liza's trust is a pour-over trust because any assets "pour over" from her will into the trust.

Grantor Annuity Trust

A <u>grantor annuity trust</u> is an irrevocable trust to which money or property is transferred in exchange for an annuity in a fixed dollar amount payable to the grantor for a specified period of time. At the end of he time period, the trust principal may be either retained in the trust or paid to other trust beneficiaries. If it is accumulated in the trust, the trust will be taxed on any income.

CASE IN POINT

Harriet Williams received $500,000 as the only beneficiary of a life insurance policy upon the death of her father. She establishes a trust with the XYZ Bank as trustee.

Under the trust agreement, the bank agrees to purchase an annuity which will pay Harriet $35,000 per year for life. The trust funds are invested in an annuity with a commercial insurance company, which guarantees that it will pay interest at the market rate and in no event less than 7 percent. Upon Harriet's death, the annuity should be worth approximately $500,000. These funds will then be distributed in equal shares to her children.

Grantor Retained Income Trust (GRIT)

A <u>grantor retained income trust</u> is specifically designed to pay trust income to the grantor for a term of years with the remaining interest passing to family members. The purpose of the trust is not to save income tax because all income is taxed to the grantor. Non-income producing or low-income producing assets with substantial appreciation potential such as real estate or stock in a closely held corporation are transferred to the grantor retained income trust.

CASE IN POINT

Janice Hill owns 100,000 shares of stock in a rapidly growing technology research company which she helped establish. The company is highly profitable and pays dividends of $.25 per share (i.e., $25,000 per year to Janice.) Janice acquired her stock for $.10 per share and it is now worth $1 per share. It is expected that it may sell for as much as $30 per share in the future. Janice transfers the stock to a trust. Under the terms of the trust agreement, Janice will be paid all trust income. Upon her death, the trust will pay all trust income in equal shares to her two children. Upon the death of her last surviving child, the trust will terminate and all funds will be equally divided among her surviving grandchildren.

Bypass Trust

A bypass trust allows married couples to avoid or reduce estate taxes.

A bypass trust allows any married couple to avoid estate tax as long as the value of their estate does not exceed $1.2 million. Any married couple whose joint assets exceed $600,000 should consider a bypass trust if they wish to reduce taxes and increase the inheritance to be received by their heirs.

When a couple uses a bypass trust, they provide that, on the death of the first spouse up to $600,000 of his or her assets will go into a trust known as a bypass, A/B, credit shelter or family trust for the surviving spouse. The surviving spouse will receive all income from the trust and will also be entitled to withdraw up to 5 percent of the trust principal annually. In addition, the trustee has the discretion to give the surviving spouse more money for any reasonable needs such as support or medical bills.

CASE IN POINT

Mark and Mary Maguire have a combined net worth of $1.5 million. Of this amount, $1 million would be includable in Mark's gross estate and the remaining $500,000 would be includable in Mary's estate. Under Mark's will, Mary will receive $400,000 outright and the remaining $600,000 will be placed in a bypass trust. The trustee is directed to pay all trust income to Mary. She would also have the right to request to be paid up to 5 percent of the trust principal annually. In addition, the trustee has the discretion to make annual distributions of principal to Mary to pay any medical bills or any unusual expenses.

The tax savings of this plan may be illustrated as follows:

| | At Mark's Death | | At Mary's Death | |
	With Bypass Trust	W/O	With Bypass Trust	W/O
Gross Estate	1,000,000	1,000,000	900,000	1,500,000
Marital Deduction	- 400,000	-1,000,000	0	0
Taxable Estate	600,000	0	900,000	1,500,00
tax	192,800	0	306,800	555,800
Unified Credit	-192,800	0	-192,800	-192,800
Tax Due	0	0	114,000	363,000

This bypass trust protects Mary because she has the right to all of the income from the trust and also to certain annual principal distributions from the trust. Further, the trustee has the discretion to provide additional funds if Mary incurs unforeseen problems requiring substantial funds. Thus, while the trust affords Mary a high level of protection, her estate will owe $249,000 less in taxes by use of this straightforward planning technique.

A QTIP Trust

A QTIP provision gives a surviving spouse a life interest in property, but does not transfer outright ownership to a surviving spouse.

A QTIP trust is one designed to maximize the estate tax marital deduction. "QTIP" refers to qualified terminable interest property. A QTIP provision gives a surviving spouse a life interest in property, but does not transfer outright ownership to a surviving spouse.

It permits the grantor of the trust to control the ultimate disposition of property. The surviving spouse must have a right to all income from the trust for life and the executor of the estate must notify the IRS of this election to treat the QTIP as qualifying for the marital deduction. Property subject to a QTIP power is includable in the estate of the surviving spouse.

CASE IN POINT

Ted, age 81, and Phyllis, age 70, were married in 1984. They both have adult children from prior marriages. Ted has owned a home at the beach for 40 years which his children and grandchildren have used and enjoyed for many years. The home is occupied by Ted's children and grandchildren from June 15 to September 1 of each year and it is rented for the remainder of the year. The home is now worth approximately $400,000.

Ted wants Phyllis to be able to enjoy the beach house as long as she is alive, but he ultimately wants it to remain the property of his children. He establishes a QTIP trust which gives Phyllis a life interest in the property and a right to all of the income from the property. If Ted's executor makes the proper election, this house will qualify for the marital deduction and will not be subject to federal estate tax at the time of his death. It will, however, be includable in Phyllis' gross estate at the time of her death.

Qualified Personal Residence Trust

A <u>Qualified Personal Residence Trust ("QPRT")</u> is a type of trust that is generally designed to transfer a primary residence or a vacation home to children (or other heirs) while reducing the size of your gross estate. As typically structured, the homeowner transfers a home to a trust. Under the terms of the trust, the person making the transfer retains the right to use the home for a specified period. At the end of this period, title to the home vests in the beneficiary (<u>i.e.</u>, your children). The former owner may retain the right to rent the property at fair market value. The person who made the transfer has made a gift equal to the present value of the remainder interest, but has removed the full value of the asset from his estate.

A qualified personal residence trust allows homeowners to transfer a home to a trust.

CASE IN POINT

Jim is 60 years old and owns a vacation home worth $400,000. He establishes a qualified personal residence trust and under the trust he retains the right to use the property for ten years. At the end of this time, the property passes to his only son. Under IRS annuity tables the value of the remainder interest is $172,076. This amount is subject to gift tax, but effectively allows Jim to remove an asset worth $400,000 from his estate at a discounted value.

If the donor dies before the term specified in the trust, the full value of the residence is included in his gross estate.

Charitable Remainder Trust

A <u>Charitable Remainder Trust</u> is designed to reduce both income and estate taxes by making a gift to charitable organizations. As typically used, the donor will give an asset (<u>i.e.</u>, house, stock, etc.) to a charity, but retain a life interest in the property. The donor and his/her spouse has the use of the asset, but it will ultimately pass to the charity. The asset is removed from the donor's taxable estate and he may also claim an immediate income tax deduction for the value of the remainder interest.

Charitable Lead Trust

A charitable lead trust allows a donor to give to a charity for a period of time, but ultimately the property reverts to children or grandchildren.

A <u>Charitable Lead Trust</u> allows a donor to make a gift of income to a charity for a period of years, but ultimately have the property revert to his children on grandchildren. Such a trust allows an individual to benefit a favorite charity, pass assets on to a loved one, and substantially reduce federal estate tax liability. Jacqueline Onassis' estate plan used a charitable lead trust to substantially reduce her potential estate tax liability.

All of the trusts discussed allow you to accomplish goals that may be important to you. Many of these trusts have the additional advantage of reducing (or avoiding) potential estate tax liability.

CHAPTER 16

Planning for Long-Term Care

Planning for Long-Term Care

The aging of our population is a topic discussed with increasing frequency in newspapers, magazines and other media. People over age 85 are the fastest growing segment of the American population. The number of people over age 65 is expected to double in the next 40 years.

For people who enjoy good mental and physical health well into their advanced years, longevity can be a blessing. For those who suffer from the mental or physical infirmities often associated with advanced age, however, longevity can create special needs and concerns. Certain of these needs and concerns may be addressed while an individual enjoys good health. Steps may be taken to ensure that the needs for physical comfort and financial security are fully met.

There are generally at least two objectives in planning for long-term care. First, one may wish to create a mechanism to permit another to act on his behalf in the event of incompetency. Second, one must ensure the availability of sufficient resources to provide for any unexpected financial burdens that stem from unanticipated health care needs.

The Need for a Substitute Decision Maker

All states recognize the authority of an individual to delegate decision-making authority to another.

Many persons fear that at some point in their lives they will no longer have the capacity to make decisions affecting their physical, emotional or financial well-being. If this concern becomes a reality, they would like to have a close friend, family member or other loved one make these decisions for them. Virtually all states recognize the authority of an individual to delegate this decision-making authority to another. (See chart on page 46.)

A durable power of attorney is a legal device by which one person authorizes another to act on his behalf in the event of incompetence. A health care power of attorney authorizes one person to make decisions regarding possible health care of the incompetent individual. A <u>living will</u> expresses a person's desire not to have life sustained through the use of extraordinary means if death appears inevitable. All of these tools are discussed in detail in Chapter 3.

Long-Term-Care Insurance[9]

The second element of planning for long term care is to ensure that a person has adequate resources to pay for the required care. Unfortunately, most people simply lack the resources to provide for costly long term care. They may, however, be able to meet these costs either through <u>long-term-care insurance</u> or <u>Medicaid.</u>

Unfortunately, most people lack the resources to provide for costly long term care.

<u>Long-term-care insurance</u> is a relatively new product. It is designed to pay the insured's bills in the event he is required to enter a nursing home or be cared for in his own home at some uncertain point in the future.

Although the products offered by insurance companies vary widely, most are one of three types: coverage for care at home, coverage for nursing home costs, and combined coverage for both at home and nursing home costs. Review any long-term-care policy carefully to ascertain which type of care will be covered.

Home-Care Coverage

The key in any home-care policy is to determine the benefits. Some policies pay home-care benefits only for the services of a licensed professional, such as a registered nurse or physical therapist. Other policies provide payment for both professional services and support services, such as cooking and housekeeping. Moreover, many such policies do not reimburse family members for performing nursing or support services. A prospective purchaser must read the fine print of a policy to make sure he is getting the benefits he expects.

---

[9] Most of the material describing long-term-care insurance is based on information in "An Empty Promise To The Elderly," *Consumer Reports* at page 425 (June 1991 ed.). Readers desiring additional information may wish to contact *Consumer Reports* for a reprint of this informative article.

Nursing-Home Coverage

The insured should carefully read any exclusions or limitations in the policy.

Policies professing to cover nursing-home care may have strict limitations on benefits. Most policies cover all levels of nursing care, including skilled, intermediate and custodial care. The insured should be especially careful to read any exclusions or limitations in the policy.

Eligibility for Benefits

All insurance policies contain provisions that address the circumstances under which its terms become operative. Long-term-care insurance policies contain restrictions on when or whether an insured is entitled to receive benefits. More liberal policies provide that the insured qualifies for benefits if his doctor orders the care. Other policies provide that benefits will be denied unless the care is medically necessary for sickness or injury. Still other policies provide that the insured must be unable to perform a specified number of "activities of daily living," such as bathing and dressing, before benefits will be paid.

Due to the varied standards used in the industry, a would-be purchaser of a long-term policy is well advised to examine these limitations carefully prior to purchasing a product.

Inflation Considerations

The buyer of any insurance policy bears a certain risk that the policy benefits may be eroded by inflation. Purchasers of long-term-care insurance incur an added risk because of the rapidly increasing costs of health care.

A limited number of carriers offer some form of inflation protection as long as the policy is in place. Although inflation protection may be expensive, it should be considered in selecting a policy.

Is the Insurer Reputable and Solvent?

A most important factor in selecting any insurance policy is the reputation and financial stability of the insurer. If there are doubts about the reputation of an insurer, one should not hesitate to check with the state insurance commissioner. Buyers should not merely assume that the salesperson is providing accurate information concerning the coverage provided and the extent of the benefits the company will pay. They must ask specific questions of the company's representative and request and carefully review the policy and other written materials that fully describe the type of coverage provided by the policy.

The financial stability of the insurer is a crucial factor. The company will only be able to provide the promised benefits if it is in business and financially solvent when any claim is made. Although there is no foolproof method to guarantee that the company one selects today will be solvent and able to pay benefits in the future, there are a few measures a purchaser can take to minimize that risk.

A purchaser should buy from a company rated "A" or "A+" by A.M. Best.

A purchaser should buy from a company rated "A" or "A+" by A. M. Best, a highly regarded authority on insurance company finances. The Best reports are available at many public libraries. Purchasers may also wish to consult such publications as *Consumer Reports* which does provide studies on long-term-care insurance.

The Role of Medicaid in Planning for Long Term Care

Cautionary Note: The trend of recent statutory enactments has been to limit eligibility for Medicaid. None of the strategies discussed in the book should be considered without the guidance of an attorney who specializes in Medicaid planning.

<u>Medicaid</u> is a health care system funded jointly by state and federal governments. It is available only to persons who are medically needy. To qualify for Medicaid coverage a person must satisfy certain asset and income criteria. In essence a person can only qualify for Medicaid if he has no funds of his own to provide for his care.

Engage in Medicaid planning only with the assistance of an attorney who specializes in Medicaid coverage.

<u>Medicaid planning</u> involves structuring an individual's finances to avoid leaving a surviving spouse bankrupt in the event of a long, costly and debilitating illness of the other spouse. The goal of Medicaid planning is to exclude assets from consideration in determining eligibility for Medicaid. This may be done by taking maximum advantage of exempt assets, and by either shifting income to the healthy spouse, or by placing assets in a Medicaid trust.

<u>The Wall Street Journal</u> has characterized Medicaid planning as one of the most controversial topics in the field of financial planning.

The authors of this book do not wish to imply that individuals either should or should not structure their financial affairs to take advantage of Medicaid coverage. Rather, the goal here is to provide certain basic information about Medicaid planning and to be responsive to the numerous questions the authors have received concerning it.

Any individual who does engage in Medicaid planning should do so with caution and only with the assistance of an attorney who specializes in Medicaid planning. There is some risk involved. In the late summer of 1996, Congress made it a crime to transfer assets in order to qualify for Medicaid assistance. At the time this book was revised, there was considerable uncertainty about how this newly enacted statute would be applied.

(Note: This provision is sometimes referred to as the "Granny Goes to Jail" law.)

Medicaid Asset Classes

Under Medicaid an individual's assets fall into one of three categories: <u>countable assets,</u> <u>exempt</u> or <u>non-countable assets</u> and <u>inaccessible assets.</u> <u>Countable assets</u> must be less than a certain minimum level for an individual to qualify for Medicaid coverage. Medicaid requires that a couple list all countable assets, regardless of whose name they are in or how long they have been in a person's name. The healthy spouse is permitted to retain a specified percentage of all assets up to a maximum level set by state law. The maximum level of assets that may be retained by a healthy spouse is indexed to inflation and is adjusted annually.

> **The healthy spouse is permitted to retain a percent of all assets up to a maximum level set by state law.**

Countable assets include bank accounts, certificates of deposit, IRAs, vacation homes, investment assets, life insurance with a cash surrender value, and any other asset that is not exempt. Exempt assets are defined by state law and often include a family home, a car, personal jewelry and household effects, a pre-paid funeral, a burial account, term life insurance and a small amount of cash. Inaccessible assets are assets once owned by an individual but no longer available because they have been given away or placed in a Medicaid Trust.

CASE IN POINT

John and Helen, a married couple, own $200,000 in jointly held assets and they each own $100,000 of assets in their individual names. John is in the early stages of Alzheimer's disease and it is expected that within the next several years he will require round-the-clock care in a nursing home at a cost of about $50,000 per year. In determining John's eligibility for Medicaid all of their assets are considered. Under the law of her state, Helen may retain $75,000 in assets and all remaining non-exempt or countable assets must be exhausted before John qualifies for Medicaid.

Income Limits

An individual seeking to qualify for Medicaid must also meet certain income requirements. These income requirements vary from state to state. Information regarding applicable income limits should be available from state Medicaid officials. If the person seeking Medicaid is married, any income attributable solely to the healthy spouse is not counted. Moreover, the income of the healthy spouse need not be used to pay nursing home costs of the spouse who is ill. If a husband and wife have joint income, the stay-at-home spouse is permitted to keep a certain amount of this joint income. In addition, most states allow an individual to exclude a personal needs allowance, a home maintenance allowance if the individual is planning to go home and an amount necessary to pay monthly health insurance premiums.

In general, a person pays the nursing home directly if his income is sufficient. If his income is not sufficient to pay nursing home expenses, Medicaid pays the difference between the person's income and the nursing home costs.

Medicaid Trusts

Individuals who wish to qualify for Medicaid may either give their assets away or place them in a Medicaid Trust.

Medicaid planning may involve a transfer of assets in an effort to reduce an individual's income or asset level to permit him to qualify for Medicaid coverage. Individuals who wish to qualify for Medicaid may either give their assets away or place them in a Medicaid Trust. Such a transfer of assets, however, starts a waiting period from 36 to 60 months before an individual will be eligible to receive Medicaid benefits. Morever, as previously noted, a person who transfers assets for the purpose of qualifying for Medicaid may face criminal sanctions.

A Medicaid Trust is an irrevocable trust designed to shield the assets or income of the person transferring assets to the trust from consideration in determining eligibility for Medicaid. The trust must be irrevocable. The trustee of a Medicaid Trust must not have the discretion to use assets for the benefit of the individual seeking Medicaid coverage. If the trustee has this discretion, it is presumed that he will exercise it and the individual will not qualify for Medicaid. This limitation on a trustee's discretion was first imposed as a result of a change in the law in 1986. Thus, any pre-1986 trust that does not limit discretion may not accomplish the goal of qualifying for Medicaid. An advantage of a Medicaid Trust is that it protects an individual's assets in the event of a long, debilitating illness that will ultimately result in death. A disadvantage is that the individual must completely surrender control of these assets. Thus, the adverse psychological impact of giving away all of one's assets might outweigh any financial advantage gained by qualifying for Medicaid.

In addition, any transfer of assets may involve tax considerations which should be discussed with a competent tax adviser and an attorney who specializes in Medicaid planning. Due to growing national concern regarding increases in the cost of health care, it is possible that federal and state awmakers may significantly curtail the use of Medicaid Trusts in the future.

CASE IN POINT

Casey Phillips is an 87-year-old widower whose health is starting to fail. His physician has advised him and his children that it would be best if he moved to a nursing home. Casey will require round-the-clock care at a cost of about $50,000 per year. His doctor indicates that while Casey has physical problems, he is mentally very keen. It is quite likely that he could live at least 10 years.

During the past 20 years Casey has made substantial gifts to his children and grandchildren and has fully used his available unified tax credit. (See Chapter 7 for discussion of this credit.)

He now owns approximately $300,000 in government bonds. The income from these bonds supplements his modest government pension and permits him to live in comfort. He is considering the advisability of transferring these bonds to a Medicaid trust so they will eventually pass to his children rather than being spent on his nursing home costs.

If Casey does transfer the bonds to a trust, he will incur a gift tax liability of approximately $87,000. In addition, both he and his children are quite concerned that the emotional impact of giving up everything he owns will be severe. He is concerned about the moral implications of sheltering his assets and placing the burden of his care on the state. Finally, it appears that if Casey does give away his assets to qualify for Medicaid, he may face criminal sanctions. While Casey may structure his affairs to qualify for Medicaid, the tax and emotional impact of this action is considerable.

Information Sources

Information regarding issues affecting long-term-care of the elderly is frequently available at either no cost or at a low cost from organizations concerned with issues affecting the elderly. These organizations include the National Council on the Aging, as well as state or local councils on aging. The address for the National Council on the Aging is 409 3rd Street, SW, Suite 200, Washington, DC 20004,(202) 479-1200. State and local offices are generally listed in local telephone directories. Information regarding insurance issues or Medicaid is generally available from state or local government agencies dealing with these issues.

Individuals needing an attorney familiar with these issues may wish to contact the National Academy of Elder Law Attorneys, 1604 North Country Club Road, Tucson, AZ 85716, (502) 811-4005, which maintains a list of attorneys practicing in the field of elder law.

Conclusion

Long-term financial planning is advisable for everyone. Planning for long-term care is especially important for persons approaching retirement or already in retirement. Long-term-care insurance and Medicaid are options that may be considered. The decision regarding the use of these options ultimately rests with the affected individual.

CHAPTER 17

The Role of Fringe Benefit Programs in Estate Planning

The Role of Fringe Benefits Programs in Estate Planning

Most government employees, whether employed at the federal, state or local level, are either required or permitted to participate in certain fringe benefit programs. These programs typically include a pension plan, a group health plan and a group life insurance plan. Although a detailed consideration of such programs is beyond the scope of this book, they do require some consideration because of their impact on estate planning.

Most government employees are either required or permitted to participate in certain fringe benefit programs.

The accrual of benefits under a pension plan alone may create a need for estate planning. The clearest illustration of this is an example provided by the Federal Retirement Thrift Investment Board, the agency that oversees the federal employee Thrift Savings Plan (TSP). The Thrift Board points out that if a federal employee earning $26,000 per year invests 5 percent of his salary in the TSP each pay period from age 20 until age 65 at a 7 percent annual return, he will have accumulated $822,900 by age 65. This is well in excess of the $600,000 level which may give rise to an estate tax liability (See Chapter 7). If the employee's salary increases beyond $26,000 per year, if he earns a higher rate of return than 7 percent, or if he increases the amount of his contribution, the accumulated amount could be significantly higher. (See Chapter 18 for further discussion of the Federal TSP.)

Pension Plans - Defined Benefit Plans

Virtually all government employers provide a pension plan for their employees. Traditionally, government pension plans have been defined benefit plans, or plans which provide a specific benefit at retirement. The amount of the benefit is based upon the retiree's years of service and earnings during employment.

Federal Civil Service Retirement System (CSRS)

The federal Civil Service Retirement System (CSRS) is an example of a typical government defined benefit plan. Under the CSRS, most federal employees are required to make non-deductible contributions equal to 7 percent of their gross salary. The employing agency matches these contributions. At retirement the employee is paid a monthly pension. The amount of the pension depends upon the employee's years of service and his compensation during a three-year base period (i.e., "the high-three" or the three consecutive years of highest compensation). Retirement benefits are paid in the form of a lifetime monthly annuity. The annuity is indexed to inflation and annual cost-of-living adjustment is

Under CSRS, most federal employees are required to make non-deductible contribution equal to 7 percent of their gross salary.

applied. If a CSRS retiree is married, he may elect a survivor annuity. When the survivor annuity is elected, the retiree's monthly annuity is decreased. Upon the retiree's death, however, the surviving spouse continues to receive a reduced annuity for life. Married retirees may decline to elect the survivor annuity, although the spouse must consent to this election.

CSRS participants also have the option of electing to contribute up to 5 percent of their salary to the TSP. These contributions are tax deductible, but the employing agency does not make a matching contribution.

State and Local Government Plans

Defined benefit programs offered by state and local governments generally require non-deductible employee contributions, and they pay pension benefits in the form of a monthly annuity. They typically provide periodic cost-of-living adjustments. The amount of a retiree's pension is based on years of service and salary during a specified base period such as the "high-three" used at the federal level. A survivor annuity is also a feature of many state and local government pension plans. A married person who wishes to decline the survivor annuity must obtain the written consent of his spouse.

The Survivor Annuity

There is a continuing debate between government actuaries and the insurance industry concerning the wisdom of choosing a survivor benefit and taking the subsequent reduction in annuity payments. Insurance industry representatives believe that it is frequently advisable to decline the survivor annuity and purchase a life insurance policy on the life of the retiree. They believe that by following this approach, the retiree will maximize his pension, save money and provide the necessary protection for the surviving spouse.

Certain government benefit experts, on the other hand, believe that with the exception of rare cases, it is financially prudent for most married employees to select the survivor benefit. The advisability of declining the spousal annuity and buying life insurance depends upon each retiree's unique situation.

An employee facing this decision needs to consider the extent to which election of the survivor annuity will reduce his annuity and how this impacts on his overall financial situation. It is essential that an individual confronted with this decision obtain unbiased professional advice.

Defined Contribution Plans

Under a typical defined contribution plan, the employee is not promised a specific retirement benefit.

A concern arose in the late 1970s that the pension liabilities of government entities were growing faster than the ability to pay them. One result of this concern was a shift in emphasis of how pension benefits would be funded. A number of governmental entities began to move away from defined benefit programs and either replaced or supplemented them with defined contribution plans.

Under a typical defined contribution plan, the employee is not promised a specific retirement benefit. Rather, the amount of the pension benefit depends upon the amount of funds contributed to the plan both by the employee and his employer and the rate of return on the invested proceeds.

Defined contribution plans typically shift the risk of providing a satisfactory pension benefit from the employer to the employee. Employees in defined contribution plans, however, may enjoy substantially greater retirement benefits depending upon the amount of their contributions and the investment of plan assets.

The Federal Employees Retirement System (FERS)

The federal retirement system was dramatically revised with the passage of the Federal Employees Retirement System Act in June, 1986, which created FERS. All federal employees hired after January 1, 1984, are subject to Social Security coverage and are required to participate in FERS.

All federal employees hired after January 1, 1984 are subject to Social Security coverage and are required to participate in FERS.

Federal employees hired prior to Jan. 1, 1984, were given the option of remaining in the Civil Service Retirement System, a defined benefit plan, or switching to the new FERS. The FERS program consists of three tiers:

- a basic annuity which is a defined benefit program similar to the CSRS but provides a much lower benefit and requires a much lower contribution (only 0.8 percent of pay);

- Social Security (See Chapter 19);

- the Thrift Savings Plan (TSP), or the defined contribution portion of the FERS program.

Upon retirement, a FERS participant becomes eligible for a basic annuity from the defined benefit tier. The amount of the annuity is based upon compensation and years of service. In addition, FERS participants are eligible to receive monthly Social Security benefits and are eligible for a number of options with respect to how the TSP portion of their retirement savings will be paid. Employees may elect to receive a lump sum payment, equal monthly payments over a specified time, a single or joint life annuity, or leave their assets in the TSP until a later time. (See Chapter 18.)

Health Insurance Programs

Without medical insurance, large estates could easily be wiped out.

Unexpected medical expenses can have a dramatic, negative impact on anyone's financial status. Medical costs hit the elderly and persons on a fixed income especially hard. *Any* financial planning must include a consideration of available medical insurance.

Without medical insurance, large estates could easily be wiped out. Virtually all government employees are fortunate because their employers provide some form of group health insurance. In addition, many of these employers permit retirees to continue their group health coverage after retirement. The availability of this coverage varies depending upon the governmental employer.

The Federal Employees Health Benefit Program (FEHB)

The Federal Employees Health Benefit program (FEHB) is the health insurance program offered to federal employees. The FEHB offers federal employees and retirees the option of enrolling in a number of separate fee-for-service plans or health maintenance organizations (HMOs). The plans available under the FEHB are group plans and the federal government pays a portion of the cost of the plan. Enrollees may change plans every year during an open season. Payment for this insurance is deducted from the employee's salary, or if retired, from the monthly annuity. Under the FEHB, an employee who has worked five consecutive years has the option of continuing health insurance coverage following retirement.

State and Local Government Health Insurance Plans

The health insurance plans offered by state and local governments vary from state to state and from county to county within a particular state. The available plans are virtually always group plans and the employing agency usually pays a portion of the cost of coverage. Some states pay as much as 100 percent of the cost of insurance, while others offer the group plan and payment is the responsibility of each employee. Many state and local government employers offer continuation coverage to retired employees.

While the cost of continuation coverage is generally shared by the government entity and the retiree, some states require retirees to pay the full amount. In many states, retiree health insurance coverage is coordinated with the availability of Medicare.

Life Insurance

Like health insurance, government employees are usually eligible to participate in group term life insurance programs during their employment and following retirement. The advantage of these programs is that they offer insurance at relatively inexpensive rates. The disadvantage, however, is that because of the limits on coverage, they may not provide sufficient coverage to provide the necessary protection. (See Chapter 10 for a discussion of the need for life insurance.)

A government employee can obtain life insurance coverage equal to five times basic pay.

Under the federal program, employees are eligible for enrollment in the Federal Employees Group Life Insurance (FEGLI) program, which they may continue into retirement. Employees may elect a number of options and the amount of insurance is generally based upon an individual's salary during employment. An individual can obtain coverage of an amount equal to five times basic pay.

The rates charged to government employees are generally attractive because the individual participates in a group plan. Group insurance is often substantially cheaper than the insurance that an employee could obtain by purchasing a policy from a private insurer.

Conclusion

An understanding of how available fringe benefits affect an individual's estate plan is essential. If these benefits are maximized, they may increase a person's net worth to a level sufficient to require professional estate and financial planning.

CHAPTER 18

Tax-Favored Estate Accumulation Techniques

Tax-Favored Estate Accumulation Techniques

The federal tax code provides encouragement to save for retirement by providing a number of incentives.

Most people hope to enjoy a financially comfortable retirement. Inheriting substantial funds or winning the lottery may be the easiest way to accomplish this objective, but few enjoy such good fortune. The best alternative for most people is to save regularly. The federal tax code provides encouragement to save for retirement by providing a number of incentives. Tax-favored <u>defined contribution plans,</u> <u>tax-sheltered annuities</u> and <u>nonqualified deferred compensation plans</u> are the most common tax-favored retirement savings option.

Retirement Plans

In the late 1970s and early 1980s when governments at all levels became concerned about their ability to pay future pension costs and began to modify existing retirement plans, they sought to move away from costs associated with defined benefit plans, to bring government employees under the Social Security system, and to give employees a larger role in planning for their retirement. New retirement systems were designed to provide benefits from three separate tiers: a defined benefit tier, a Social Security tier and a defined contribution tier, a tier requiring greater employee contributions toward retirement.

Like benefits payable under defined benefit *plans,* benefits payable under defined benefit *tiers* are based upon years of service and compensation; however, the benefits provided under defined benefit tiers are substantially less generous than under defined benefit plans. The Social Security tier and the defined contribution tier are expected to supplement the benefits received under the defined benefit tier.

Social Security benefits are the same as those available to any person covered by Social Security. (See Chapter 19 for a discussion of Social Security.) Benefits available under the defined contribution tier vary depending upon the amount of funds contributed by the employee, any employer matching contributions, and the investment performance of any invested funds. (See pages 178-184.)

At the federal level, the change in the retirement program was implemented by the passage of the Federal Employees Retirement System Act of 1986. Similar retirement system changes have also been implemented by many state and local governments. While existing employees are generally given the option of remaining in a defined benefit plan, newly hired employees are usually required to participate in the newly established plans.

Defined Contribution Plans

The movement away from defined benefit plans may have eliminated the certainty in determining the amount of an employee's retirement benefit; however, implementation of the defined contribution feature of redesigned pension plans offer a number of significant advantages.

Participants are given more control over the accumulation of funds for retirement by deciding how much to contribute and the right to select the type of investment.

Participants are given more control over the accumulation of funds for retirement by deciding how much to contribute and by being given the right to select the type of investment for their retirement funds (e.g., stocks or bonds). In addition, tax incentives never previously available, including the right to make tax-deductible contributions and to receive tax-favored distributions from the plan, are made available. Persons who consistently save even a modest amount under a typical defined contribution plan may accumulate in excess of $1 million during a government career.

The Federal Thrift Savings Plan

The Federal Thrift Savings Plan is the defined contribution plan available to employees of the federal government. It was enacted as part of the FERS Act, and a significant portion of the retirement benefit under FERS is provided through the TSP. Virtually all federal employees, including participants in the CSRS, are eligible to participate in the TSP; however, greater incentives are available for employees who are participants in the FERS.

Both FERS and CSRS participants in the TSP may exclude their TSP contributions from income tax, and they may choose which of three investment funds and in what amounts their contributions should be invested. Their investment options include a short term government securities fund, a common stock index fund, and a long-term bond fund which invests in both corporate and government bonds. All assets are managed by the Thrift Savings Board.

FERS Employees Matching Contributions

FERS participants receive a matching contribution from their employer on a one-for-two basis.

Under the TSP, a FERS employee may elect to make tax deductible contributions of up to 10 percent of his salary, not to exceed $9,500 in 1997. The maximum dollar contribution an employee may make is indexed and increases each year, but may not exceed 10 percent of salary.

A contribution of 1 percent of salary is made to the TSP account of all FERS participants (but not persons covered by CSRS) by the employing agency, regardless of whether the employee elects to contribute to the TSP.

FERS participants (not CSRS) also receive a <u>matching contribution</u> from their employer on a one-for-two basis. The amount of the matching contribution is as follows:

Employee Contribution	Automatic Contribution	Agency Matching Contribution	Total Contribution
0 Percent	1 Percent	0 Percent	1 Percent
1 Percent	1 Percent	1 Percent	3 Percent
2 Percent	1 Percent	2 Percent	5 Percent
3 Percent	1 Percent	3 Percent	7 Percent
4 Percent	1 Percent	3.5 Percent	8.5 Percent
5 Percent	1 Percent	4 Percent	10 Percent
6-10 Percent	1 Percent	4 Percent	11-15 Percent

In other words, for every two dollars contributed to the TSP by the employee, the employer makes a matching contribution of one additional dollar. Thus, if an employee elects to defer 10 percent of his salary, the federal government contributes an additional 5 percent.

CASE IN POINT

Sally Clark is an attorney in the Justice Department earning $70,000 per year. She elects to contribute 10 percent of her salary to the TSP and her employer makes a 5 percent matching contribution. Thus, a total of $10,500 is contributed to the TSP on Sally's behalf, $7,000 by her and the remaining $3,500 by the Justice Department. The $9,500 contribution limit only applies to Sally's personal contribution and is not applicable to any matching contribution. Since all contributions to the TSP are tax deductible, Sally's taxable income is reduced by $7,000, the amount of her personal contribution. The matching contribution is not included in Sally's current taxable income.

Civil Service Retirement System

Participants in the federal CSRS are also eligible to elect to participate in the TSP; however, because the CSRS is a pure defined benefit plan and consequently substantially more generous than the defined benefit tier of FERS, the ability of CSRS covered employees to contribute to the TSP is limited. CSRS participants may elect to defer up to 5 percent of salary, but they are not eligible for agency matching contributions.

CSRS participants may elect to defer up to 5 percent of salary, but they are not eligible for agency matching contributions.

CASE IN POINT

Sara Williams, a mid-level manager at the Department of Agriculture with an annual salary of $55,900, is a participant in the CSRS, not the FERS. If she wishes to contribute the maximum allowable amount to the TSP, she may contribute only 5 percent of her salary, or $2,795. She is not eligible for any matching contributions.

Vesting

<u>Vesting</u> means that a retirement plan participant has met the requirements that entitle him to the funds in his retirement account upon termination of employment. Both FERS and CSRS participants in the TSP are always vested in their own contributions and any earnings on these contributions. In addition FERS participants are always vested in their agencies' matching contributions and any earnings on them. Most FERS employees become vested in the automatic 1 percent contribution within three years of service.

Tax Advantages of Participation in the TSP

Tax savings provide a significant incentive for an individual to contribute the maximum amount to the TSP. Neither employee contributions to the TSP nor agency matching contributions are included in an individual's federal or state taxable income. TSP contributions are, however, subject to Social Security tax. Any income earned on contributions to the TSP is tax deferred, meaning funds in the TSP only become taxable when they are ultimately distributed to a plan participant.

Funds in the TSP only become taxable when they are ultimately distributed to a plan participant.

A plan participant may leave funds in the TSP until the later of age 70 1/2 or until separation from government service. In most instances, a person will begin receiving funds from the TSP when he retires. At retirement, he may take his funds in either a lump sum, in equal monthly payments over a specified time period, or as a single or joint life annuity.

When a TSP participant leaves government service, but is not retiring, he may elect to receive payment of his entire vested balance in his TSP account in a lump sum or leave the funds in the TSP until age 70 1/2. If this lump sum election is made, it may qualify for additional tax benefits, such as income averaging or a tax free roll-over to an individual retirement account, where withdrawals need not begin until age 70 1/2.

CASE IN POINT

George and Helen Harrison are husband and wife. They are both employees of the federal government and both participate in the FERS program. George is an ecologist with the Department of the Interior with an annual salary of $68,129. Helen is a lawyer with the Internal Revenue Service. Her annual salary is $71,918. They are in the combined 35 percent federal/state tax bracket. George contributes 10 percent of his salary, or $6,813, to the TSP in 1997. The Interior Department makes a 5 percent matching contribution of $3,406. The total amount contributed to George's account in 1997 is $10,219. Helen also makes the maximum 10 percent contribution of $7,192 to her TSP account in 1997 and the IRS makes a 5 percent matching contribution of $3,596. The total amount contributed to Helen's account in 1997 is $10,788. The total contributions from all sources for George and Helen in 1997 is $21,007.

George and Helen have made total personal contributions of $14,005. Since their combined federal/state tax bracket is 35 percent, these contributions will save them $4,902 in taxes (i.e., 35 percent x $14,005) in 1997. The net after tax cost of these contributions to George and Helen is $9,103 (i.e., $14,005 - $4,902). Thus, the total contributions to their TSP accounts during 1997 were $21,007, and the net after tax cost to them is only $9,103.

Investment Options

Participants in the TSP may invest in one of three separate funds, the C Fund, the F Fund or the G Fund. The C Fund is a common stock fund which invests in a diverse portfolio of common stocks. Its performance is designed to match the Standard & Poor's 500 stock index. The C Fund provides the highest level of risk over a short period, but also provides the greatest possibility of a long-term return. The F Fund is a bond fund which invests in long-term obligations that provide a fixed rate of return. It is less volatile that the C Fund, but it is likely to provide a lower rate of return over the long term.

TSP participants may invest in the C Fund, the F Fund or the G Fund.

The G Fund is the most stable of the three funds because it invests in short-term government obligations but under the law receives long-term rates of return. While the G Fund promises a fixed-rate of return, in the long run the total return is likely to be less than either the C or F Funds. The Federal Retirement Thrift Investment Board has reported the relative performance of the C, F and G Funds since inception as follows:

Year	C Fund	F Fund	G Fund
1987	—	—	6.42%
1988	11.84%**	6.63%**	8.81%
1989	31.03%	13.89%	8.81%
1990	(3.15%)	8.00%	8.90%
1991	30.77%	15.75%	8.15%
1992	7.70%	7.20%	7.23%
1993	10.13%	9.52%	6.14%
1994	1.33%	(2.96%)	7.22%
1995	37.41%	18.31%	7.03%
1996	22.85%	3.66%	6.76%

** January 28, 1988, to year end
Percentages in ( ) are negative.

It is, of course, uncertain how the TSP funds will perform over longer time periods, but similar private sector funds during the 50-year period from 1939 through 1988 performed as follows:[10]

Time Period	S&P 500	Long Term Government Bonds	Treasury Bills
1979 - 1988	16.3%	10.6%	9.1%
1969 - 1988	9.5%	7.8%	7.5%
1959 - 1988	9.7%	5.8%	6.2%
1949 - 1988	12.2%	4.5%	5.0%
1939 - 1988	11.2%	4.2%	4.1%

The S&P 500 is comparable to the C Fund, the long-term government bonds to the F Fund, and Treasury bills to the G Fund.

[10] Source: Ibbotsen and Sinquefield, "Stocks, Bonds, Bills and Inflation." 1982 ed., Institute of Chartered Financial Analysis, Charlottesville, VA; updated by Ibbotsen Associates, "Stocks, Bonds, Bills and Inflation." 1998 Yearbook, Chicago, IL.

Estate Accumulation

Consistent investment in the TSP not only results in significant tax savings, but it also results in the accumulation of substantial amounts of money during a government career. This is illustrated by an example offered by the Federal Retirement Thrift Savings Board. If an individual contributes $50 per pay period (every two weeks) to the TSP, he may accumulate more than $1 million during his government career.

The chart below shows what the account balance of an individual contributing $50 every two weeks would be at three different interest rates in five year intervals.

Account Balance at Assumed Annual Rates of Return[11]
(Compounded Monthly)

Account Balance	4 Percent	7 Percent	10 Percent
5 Years	$ 14,300	$ 15,600	$ 16,900
10 Years	31,980	37,440	44,460
15 Years	53,300	68,900	89,960
20 Years	79,560	113,100	164,840
25 Years	111,540	175,760	288,080
30 Years	150,540	264,680	490,880
35 Years	198,120	390,780	824,460
40 Years	256,360	569,660	1,373,320

The Federal Retirement Thrift Savings Board has also prepared the following three tables to help employees estimate what their TSP account would accumulate using certain assumptions. To use the charts, select a table based upon the desired rate of return 4 percent, 7 percent or 10 percent each year. Choose the percentage of pay that will be contributed to the TSP account each pay period and the number of years during which it will be contributed. Find the figure in the column and row that corresponds to these choices. Multiply current annual basic pay by this figure. The result will be the expected TSP balance at the end of the chosen period for:

[11] Source: Federal Thrift Savings Investment Board, "Summary of the Thrift Savings Plan for Federal Employees," September 1990.

- A FERS employee with

- no additional salary increases, and assuming

- employee contributions and agency's contributions accrue earnings at the annual rate (compounded monthly) specified at the top of the appropriate table.

CSRS employees should use the footnotes to the tables to determine which column(s) to use.

Factors to Estimate Thrift Savings Plan Account Balance
(When Multiplied by Annual Salary)

If Investment Income Is Earned at 4% Annual Rate of Return (Compounded Monthly)

Years You Contribute	If You Contribute One of These Percentages										
	0%*	1%*	2%**	3%	4%	5%	6%	7%	8%	9%	10%
5	0.06	0.17	0.28	0.39	0.47	0.55	0.61	0.66	0.72	0.77	0.83
10	0.12	0.37	0.61	0.86	1.04	1.23	1.35	1.47	1.60	1.72	1.84
15	0.21	0.62	1.03	1.44	1.74	2.05	2.26	2.46	2.67	2.87	3.08
20	0.31	0.92	1.53	2.14	2.60	3.06	3.37	3.67	3.98	4.28	4.59
25	0.43	1.29	2.14	3.00	3.65	4.29	4.72	5.15	5.57	6.00	6.43
30	0.58	1.74	2.89	4.05	4.92	5.79	6.37	6.95	7.53	8.10	8.68
35	0.76	2.29	3.81	5.33	6.48	7.62	8.38	9.15	9.91	10.67	11.43
40	0.99	2.96	4.93	6.90	8.38	9.86	10.84	11.83	12.82	13.80	14.79

If Investment Income Is Earned at 7% Annual Rate of Return (Compounded Monthly)

Years You Contribute	If You Contribute One of These Percentages										
	0%*	1%*	2%**	3%	4%	5%	6%	7%	8%	9%	10%
5	0.06	0.18	0.30	0.42	0.51	0.60	0.66	0.72	0.78	0.84	0.90
10	0.14	0.43	0.72	1.01	1.23	1.44	1.59	1.73	1.88	2.02	2.17
15	0.26	0.79	1.32	1.85	2.25	2.65	2.91	3.17	3.44	3.70	3.97
20	0.43	1.30	2.17	3.04	3.70	4.35	4.78	5.22	5.65	6.09	6.52
25	0.68	2.03	3.38	4.73	5.75	6.76	7.44	8.11	8.79	9.47	10.14
30	1.02	3.05	5.09	7.13	8.66	10.18	11.20	12.22	13.24	14.26	15.27
35	1.50	4.51	7.52	10.52	12.78	15.03	16.54	18.04	19.54	21.05	22.55
40	2.19	6.57	10.95	15.34	18.62	21.91	24.10	26.29	28.48	30.67	32.86

If Investment Income Is Earned at 10% Annual Rate of Return (Compounded Monthly)

Years You Contribute	If You Contribute One of These Percentages										
	0%*	1%*	2%**	3%	4%	5%	6%	7%	8%	9%	10%
5	0.06	0.19	0.32	0.45	0.55	0.65	0.71	0.78	0.84	0.91	0.97
10	0.17	0.51	0.86	1.20	1.45	1.71	1.88	2.05	2.22	2.40	2.57
15	0.35	1.04	1.73	2.42	2.94	3.46	3.81	4.15	4.50	4.85	5.19
20	0.63	1.90	3.17	4.44	5.39	6.34	6.98	7.61	8.24	8.88	9.51
25	1.11	3.32	5.54	7.76	9.42	11.08	12.19	13.30	14.41	15.51	16.62
30	1.89	5.66	9.44	13.22	16.05	18.88	20.77	22.66	24.54	26.43	28.32
35	3.17	9.51	15.85	22.20	26.95	31.71	34.88	38.05	41.22	44.39	47.56
40	5.28	15.85	26.41	36.97	44.90	52.82	58.10	63.38	68.66	73.95	79.23

* or CSRS employee contributing 1%   ** or CSRS employee contributing 3%   *** or CSRS employee contributing 5%

Note: These factors are based on biweekly payroll contributions. Figures are rounded to two decimal places.

The use of these charts may be illustrated by the following examples.

CASE IN POINT

Ruth Champion is a 35-year-old federal government computer programmer with an annual salary of $42,266. She plans to remain a federal employee until she reaches age 65. She is a FERS employee and plans to make the maximum (10 percent) contribution to the TSP. If Ruth assumes that her salary will remain the same for the duration of her federal employment and she is able to invest these funds at a 10 percent rate of return, her Thrift Savings Account will be worth $1,196,973 at the time of her retirement.

CASE IN POINT

Matt McMillan is a 21-year-old employee with the Department of Defense who plans to work for the federal government for 35 years. His annual salary is $31,116; he intends to contribute 5 percent of his salary ($59.83 per pay period) to the TSP. If Matt remains employed for 35 years, if his TSP contributions remain constant at $59.83 every two weeks, and if he realizes a 10 percent annual return on his investment, he will have $986,688 in his account by the time he retires at age 56. If he waits to retire until he is 61 and has 40 years of government service, he will have $1,643,547 in his TSP account. If his salary increases and his 5 percent contribution is more than $59.83, his total obviously will be more.

CASE IN POINT

James Gregory is a 50-year-old Senior Executive Service employee whose salary is $100,500. He is a CSRS participant who elects to defer 5 percent of his salary. He intends to remain employed until he reaches age 65.

James will have a balance of $173,865 in his account at that time if his salary remains the same and if he realizes an annual return on his investment of 10 percent.

Loan Features

A participant in the TSP is permitted to borrow from the vested balance in his account. The minimum loan amount is $1,000; the maximum amount depends on the amount the employee has contributed, but may not exceed $50,000. The rate of interest on the loan is the current rate of interest on the G Fund. All interest payments are made to the employee's own account.

State and Local Government Tax-Favored Plans

State and local governments also sponsor a variety of tax-qualified defined contribution plans similar to the Federal Thrift Savings Plan.

State and local governments also sponsor a variety of tax-qualified defined contribution plans with features similar to those of the Federal Thrift Savings Plan. Because of the diversity of these plans, a detailed discussion of any one of them is beyond the scope of this publication.

The tax code does, however, authorize state or local government employers to establish non-qualified deferred compensation plans which offer certain tax-favored benefits similar to those available to federal employees under the TSP. If the plan is structured in accordance with the provisions of the tax code, any contributions to it are excluded from taxable income.

Under a non-qualified deferred compensation plan a participant may annually defer the lesser of $7,500 or 33 1/3 percent of currently includable compensation.

Currently includable compensation is total compensation reduced by the amount deferred. Stated more simply, the contribution limit is 25 percent of the participant's total compensation.

CASE IN POINT

Jeanine Phillips is employed as a teacher in a school district which has a non-qualified deferred compensation plan. Her salary is $25,000 and she wishes to defer the maximum amount possible. She may elect to defer $6,250. This amount is 25 percent of her total compensation, but it is 33 1/3 percent of her currently includable compensation ($18,750). Currently includable compensation is her total compensation ($25,000), less the amount she elected to defer ($6,250) or $18,750.

Catch Up Provision

An additional catch-up provision is permitted for persons who participate in a nonqualified deferred compensation plan of a state or local government employer. A person is eligible for this catch-up if he is within three (3) years of the plan's normal retirement age and has not made the maximum allowable contribution in prior years. The maximum amount that can be deferred in the catch-up year is $15,000.

CASE IN POINT

In 1997 Herman Hilliard, a 62-year-old eligible participant in a non-qualified deferred compensation plan with a normal retirement age of 65, received a salary of $20,000. He had been a plan participant for four years, and he had total unused contributions from prior plan years in the total amount of $15,000.

He may elect to use the catch-up provision in 1997 and defer up to $15,000. This represents his 1997 contribution of $5,000 (i.e., $20,000 x 25 percent) plus his catch-up contribution of $10,000. At the end of 1997 he will have unused contributions of $5,000. Thus, he may contribute at least $5,000 in 1998 by again taking advantage of the catch-up provision.

Tax-Sheltered Annuities

A public school system or an educational organization may provide retirement benefits for its employees through a <u>tax sheltered annuity</u> program. If the plan is properly structured, employees may defer a portion of their salary and have it contributed to the plan. The deferred amounts are not included in the income of the employees and any earnings are not currently taxable. There is a complex formula for determining the maximum amount which may be contributed on behalf of an employee in any given year. This formula is based upon an employee's years of service and contributions to the plan during prior covered employment. The maximum limit on an elective deferral in any one year is the lesser of 25 percent of compensation or $30,000. Benefits counselors in a school system are generally available to explain the specific amount that may be deferred.

Tax-Deferred Annuities

There is no limit on the amount that may be contributed to a tax-deferred annuity.

<u>Tax-deferred annuities</u> provide another widely available option for persons seeking to save funds for retirement through tax-favored investment vehicles. They are available to any individual and are not related to employment or income levels. Tax-deferred annuities can be purchased through banks, insurance companies or mutual fund companies.

The person purchasing the annuity has the option of investing in stocks, bonds or other types of investments.

There is no limit on the amount that may be contributed to a tax-deferred annuity. Contributions are not tax deductible; however, income earned on funds invested in the annuity is not subject to tax until it is distributed.

When a person begins taking distributions from the annuity, a portion of each distribution is tax free to the extent it represents a refund of his previously taxed contributions.

Because contributions to tax-deferred annuities are not deductible, it is advisable to maximize available tax deductible contributions under an employer-sponsored plan before contributing to a tax-deferred annuity.

Early Withdrawal Penalties

All of the tax-favored arrangements discussed in this chapter are designed to be long-term investments. If any amounts contributed to these programs are withdrawn prior to age 59 1/2, regular taxes must be paid and a 10 percent tax penalty may also be imposed on the taxable portion of the early distribution. There are a number of detailed exceptions which permit penalty-free withdrawals prior to age 59 1/2. Common exceptions include payments to a person who is at least 55 after separation from service, payments made by reason of disability, or payments made on account of the death of the annuitant or plan participant.

Early withdrawal penalties may be avoided by taking advantage of any loan features which may be available as part of a qualified plan. Penalty-free loans from a tax-deferred annuity are not available.

A person who needs to withdraw funds prior to age 59 may find it advisable to consult either the Internal Revenue Service or a tax adviser to determine whether there are any circumstances that would permit a penalty-free withdrawal.

Withdrawls from a tax deferred plan prior to age 59 1/2 may be subject to a 10% penalty.

In addition, tax-deferred annuities purchased through private companies may also carry certain fees or penalties on funds withdrawn prior to the time specified in the annuity contract. For example, Company A, an insurance company offers a variety of tax-deferred annuities. According to the annuity contract, if a person makes a withdrawal within 10 years of making his original investment, a premature withdrawal penalty will be imposed. If the withdrawal is made during the first year, the amount of the penalty is 10 percent. This penalty is reduced by 1 percent per year. Thus, if a person makes a withdrawal after seven years the penalty is 3 percent.

Because of the penalties on early withdrawal, funds contributed to a tax-favored plan should be those which will not be needed in the short term.

Conclusion

The widespread availability of tax-favored retirement arrangements offers most government employees an opportunity to accumulate substantial estates during the course of their careers. A person who starts saving early and is consistent in continuing to save may well retire with more than $1 million in his retirement accounts.

CHAPTER 19

Social Security and Medicare

Social Security and Medicare

Full Social Security benefits are payable to qualified workers when they reach the age of 65.

Social Security is a social insurance program based on the principle that society as a whole should protect its working population against the loss of income due to retirement, disability, and survivor benefits. Most state and local government employees and all federal employees enrolled in FERS are covered by Social Security. Federal employees covered by the CSRS are not eligible for Social Security unless they have qualified for coverage through other employment. Government employees who are not covered by Social Security may also obtain coverage through their spouses.

Social Security coverage may be an important element in any estate or financial plan. Information regarding the availability of Social Security benefits may be obtained from one of the more than 1,300 district or branch offices of the Social Security Administration. The telephone number and address of local offices may be obtained from any telephone directory. In addition, the Social Security Administration has a toll free number (1-800-772-1213) to assist individuals seeking information about Social Security or Medicare benefits.

How Social Security Works

Employers, employees and self-employed individuals are required to pay Social Security taxes during their working years. These taxes are used to provide benefits for the disabled and their survivors, and for retirees and their survivors.

Full Social Security benefits are payable to qualified workers when they reach age 65. Eligible individuals may choose to receive Social Security benefits as early as age 62.

The amount of the monthly benefit is reduced, however, for any person who starts receiving benefits prior to age 65. The amount of the reduction depends upon the recipient's age at the time he starts receiving benefits. When a person retires under Social Security, a spouse over age 60 and certain minor or disabled children may also be eligible for a monthly benefit.

When a person covered by Social Security dies, a minimal lump sum payment of $255 is paid to certain survivors. In addition, unmarried children of a decedent under age 18, disabled children, or the widow or widower of the decedent may also be eligible for a monthly survivor benefit.

Social Security Eligibility

To be entitled to Social Security benefits, an individual must work for a specified time, which is generally forty (40) calendar quarters (10 years) under Social Security. In addition, individuals born prior to 1929 may be eligible for Social Security benefits if they have less than forty (40) quarters of covered employment. Questions regarding eligibility should be directed to the nearest Social Security Administration office.

Tax Rates

All wages up to a maximum of $65,400 per year in 1997 are subject to the Social Security tax even if the person already receives Social Security benefits. This wage level is indexed to inflation and changes annually. Employers and employees pay an equal share of the tax. Self-employed persons pay both the employer and employee share.

In 1997 employers and employees each pay 7.65 percent on their earned income. (6.2 percent is attributed to Social Security tax on the first $65,400 of earned income and 1.45 percent is attributed to Medicare tax on any amount of earned income.) The maximum Social Security tax liability for 1994 is $4,054.80. There is no maximum limit for Medicare tax.

CASE IN POINT

Phil is employed by ABC Company at a salary of $70,000 per year. In 1997, he will pay 7.65 percent (i.e., 6.2 percent Social Security tax and 1.45 percent Medicare tax) of his salary on the first $65,400 of his income, or $5,003.10. Phil's income in excess of $65,400 is not subject to Social Security tax, but it is subject to Medicare tax in the amount of $66.70 ($70,000 - $65,400 = $4,600 x 1.45 percent.) Thus, Phil pays a total of $5,069.80 ($5,003.10 + $ 66.70.) His employer pays a similar amount.

Social Security Benefit Calculations

Average indexed monthly earnings or AIME is a figure that boils an individual's lifetime Social Security coverage down to one month.

Social Security retirement benefits are calculated by reviewing actual wages earned during Social Security-covered employment, indexing these wages so they reflect the impact of economic changes over time (i.e., inflation) and averaging the indexed wages.

When this process is completed the resulting figure is the <u>average indexed monthly earnings</u> or <u>AIME.</u> In essence, AIME boils an individual's lifetime Social Security coverage down to one month.

Once a person's AIME is determined his <u>Primary Insurance Amount (PIA),</u> or monthly benefit, is determined by a legally mandated formula. For a person who reaches age 62 in 1997, this formula requires that the person multiplies his first $455 of AIME by 90 percent; the next $2,286 (i.e., the amount between $455 and $2,741) by 32 percent, and any amount in excess of $2,741 by 15 percent. These divisions are known as <u>bend points.</u> The dollar amounts change annually, but the percentages are established in the law.

CASE IN POINT

Edward Daley became 62 in 1997. His average indexed monthly earnings (AIME) were $3,000. His monthly Social Security benefit is computed as follows:

Determining a person's AIME can be a tedious process. An individual must know:

- All his wages subject to Social Security each year since he started Social Security-covered employment.

90%	x	455	=	$ 409.50
32%	x	2,286	=	731.52
15%	x	259	=	38.85
PIA			=	$ 1,179.87

- The maximum wage base level in each year of Social Security covered employment. The maximum wage base level is the maximum amount of earnings subject to Social Security tax in a given year. The maximum level is adjusted annually and for 1997 is $65,400.

- The appropriate index figure for each year.

The Social Security Administration has provided a much easier alternative. It will provide an estimate of monthly benefits for those who complete SSA Form 7004, Request for Earnings and Benefits Statement. A copy of this form may be obtained by calling 1-800-772-1213.

Spousal and Survivor Benefits

Many government employees were not covered by Social Security until recent changes in government retirement systems. A government retiree who did not earn Social Security benefits during government employment may, however, be eligible for benefits based on his spouse's Social Security coverage (the spousal benefit). If a person is eligible for spousal benefit and begins taking this benefit at age 65, it will equal 50 percent of the amount the covered spouse receives. If an eligible individual elects to receive a spousal benefit beginning at age 62, the benefit will be 37.5 percent of the amount the covered spouse receives. *For qualified spouses the spousal benefit is paid in addition to the earned Social Security benefit.*

A government retiree who did not earn Social Security benefits may be eligible for benefits based on the spousal benefit.

Case In Point

Charlie Higgins is a retired government employee and his wife, Ann, is retired from a full career in the private sector. Charlie was not covered by Social Security, but Ann was. She now receives a monthly Social Security benefit of $850. At age 62 Charlie may qualify for a Social Security spousal benefit of $318.75 (i.e., $850 x 37.5 percent). If he is age 65 or older, his monthly spousal benefit will be $425 (i.e., $850 x 50 percent).

The maximum Social Security benefit in 1994 for an individual over age 65 is $1,147 per month, while the average monthly Social Security benefit for such an individual is $674 per month. Social Security benefits are adjusted annually to reflect any increase in the Consumer Price Index.

Tax Status of Social Security Benefits

Starting in 1984 Social Security benefits became taxable for certain retirees. Up to one-half of Social Security benefits will be taxed if the modified adjusted gross income of a single individual exceeds $25,000, or if the modified adjusted gross income of a married couple filing jointly exceeds $32,000. Effective January 1, 1994, 85 percent of Social Security benefits will be taxed if the modified adjusted gross income of a married couple exceeds $44,000, or if the modified adjusted gross income of a single individual exceeds $34,000. The instructions accompanying the federal income tax forms include a worksheet to be used to compute the taxable portion of a Social Security benefit.

Social Security and Post-Retirement Income

There is no limit on the income which may be earned by an individual who is 70 years or older.

If an individual under the age of 65 continues to work and earns more than $8,640 in 1997, he may be subject to a reduction in his Social Security benefit. Similarly, an individual between the ages of 65 and 69 may receive a reduced Social Security benefit if he continues to work and earns more than $13,500 in 1997. There is no limit on the income which may be earned by an individual who is 70 or older.

Social Security and Government Employees

Two particular provisions of the Social Security laws apply to government employees and impact significantly on a retiree's benefits. These provisions are the windfall eliminations provision and the government pension offset. If either of these provisions applies, the amount of the

Social Security benefit payable to government retirees or their survivors is reduced.

Government Pension Offset

The government pension offset affects persons who receive a pension from a federal, state or local government and who also qualify for a Social Security benefit based on their spouse's employment. This offset reduces or eliminates the amount of the spousal benefit payable to the government retiree. The Social Security benefit is reduced by $2 for every $3 of government pension. Stated differently, two-thirds of the government retiree's pension will be applied to offset the amount of his spousal Social Security benefit.

CASE IN POINT

Roger and Anne Wylie, husband and wife, are both 62 years of age. Roger had been employed by the federal government for 35 years when he retired at age 60. He receives a monthly annuity of $2,300. Anne worked for 30 years in a number of jobs and became eligible for a Social Security benefit of $578 per month when she retired. Roger would be eligible for a Social Security spousal benefit of $216.75, (i.e., 37.5 percent x $578) based on Anne's Social Security benefit; however, this benefit is offset by the amount of Roger's monthly annuity.

Since two-thirds of Roger's annuity (2/3 x $2,300 = $1,534.10) is more than his Social Security spousal benefit, he will not receive any Social Security benefit.

Persons Exempt from the Government Pension Offset[12]

The government pension offset does not apply in the following circumstances:

• If the individual's government pension is based on his own Social Security-covered employment. This would include any government em-

---

[12] These exemptions were taken from Social Security Administration Publication No. 05-100007 (Nov. 1991), "Government Pension Offset." The publication is available upon request and may be obtained by calling 1-800-772-1213.

ployment during which the person paid the Social Security tax. (Note: The windfall eliminations provision may, however, still apply. See the following discussion.)

• If a person receives a government pension that is not based on his/her earnings. For example, if a person receives a survivor annuity from the federal government based upon his deceased spouse's government employment, the amount of the survivor annuity does not offset any Social Security benefit;

• Anyone who either received or who was eligible to receive a government pension before December 1982, and who met all requirements for the Social Security spousal benefits in effect in January 1977;

• Anyone who receives or was eligible to receive a government pension before July 1, 1983, and was receiving one-half support from his/her spouse;

• Federal employees who are mandatorily covered by Social Security. Thus, the government pension offset does not apply to FERS-covered employees;

• Federal employees who chose to switch from the Civil Service Retirement System to Social Security-covered employment on or before December 31, 1987.

The Windfall Elimination Provision

The purpose behind the windfall provision is to keep full career government employees from taking advantage of the Social Security tilt.

The windfall elimination provision reduces Social Security benefits to persons who receive a government annuity (federal, state, and local) and who do not have a full career under Social Security (less than 30 years at a more than nominal salary, or about $10,000 per year). Persons typically affected include individuals who have worked some years in private sector and qualified for Social Security, but the bulk of their careers was in a government position not covered by Social Security. The provision applies to anyone who becomes 62 (or disabled) after 1985 and becomes eligible for a government annuity after 1985. Both must occur after 1985.

Social Security is designed to pay larger benefits in relation to earnings to lower-paid workers than to higher-paid persons. This is referred to as the Social Security tilt. The purpose behind the windfall provision is to keep full-career government employees, most of whom have full careers at adequate salaries or above, from taking advantage of the Social Security tilt. An individual who pays Social Security taxes for only a few years or only a portion of his career will fall statistically among full-career, lower-paid workers. As such, the worker receives a proportionally larger benefit from Social Security than mid-to-upper income employees.

So that government annuitants do not receive benefits designed for low-income, full-career Social Security recipients, government annuitants who became 62 in 1990 (and were not eligible for a federal annuity until after 1985) will have their Social Security benefit decreased by about 50 percent. (Persons who turned 62 in 1986 through 1989 are reduced by a lower amount.) An additional 20 percent is deducted if a person takes his benefit at age 62 rather than waiting for full retirement at age 65. The total reduction, however, cannot be more than one-half of the amount of the government annuity.

Social Security is designed to pay larger benefits in relation to earnings to lower-paid workers than to higher-paid persons.

Mechanical Application of the Windfall Elimination Provision

The windfall elimination provision works by changing the first factor used in computing the monthly Social Security benefit, or PIA. (See discussion in this Chapter for an explanation of how the PIA is calculated.) If the individual has 20 or fewer years of Social Security-covered employment, the first $455 of average indexed monthly earnings (AIME) is multiplied by 40 percent, rather than by 90 percent (the figure used for those with a full Social Security career, 30 or more years of Social Security-covered employment). The actual effect of this formula is that a person's monthly benefit may be reduced by a maximum of $227.50 per month, or $2,730 per year.

The effect of the windfall elimination provision is lessened if an individual has more than 20 but less than 30 years of substantial Social Security earnings (i.e., more than $10,000 per year). The first bend point is reduced as follows:

Years of Social Security Earnings	First Bend Point
30 or more	90 percent
29	85 percent
28	80 percent
27	75 percent
26	70 percent
25	65 percent
24	60 percent
23	55 percent
22	50 percent
21	45 percent
20 or less	40 percent

Case In Point

If Edward Daley (the person referred to earlier in this Chapter) has 22 years of Social Security-covered employment but is subject to the windfall elimination provision, this would reduce his monthly Social Security benefit. In computing his Social Security benefit, the first $455 of monthly Social Security coverage will be multiplied by 50 percent (rather than 90 percent); it will equal $211. Edward's monthly benefit or PIA is then computed as follows:

50%	x	455	=	$ 227.50
32%	x	2,286	=	731.52
15%	x	259	=	38.85
PIA			=	$ 997.87

Accordingly, his monthly benefit would be $997.87, or $182.00 per month less than if the windfall provision did not apply. Thus, because the windfall elimination provision applies to Edward, his Social Security benefit is reduced by $2,184.00 per year (i.e., 12 months x $182.00.)

If Edward were to remain employed in a Social Security-covered position for three more years (25 total years) his PIA would be computed as follows:

This illustrates that by continuing Social Security-covered employment, a person may reduce the impact of the windfall elimination provision, assuming all other factors remain constant.

65%	x	455	=	$ 295.75
32%	x	2,286	=	731.52
15%	x	259	=	38.85
PIA			=	$ 1,006.12

Persons Exempt from Windfall Elimination Provision[13]

Persons exempt from the windfall elimination provision include:

- Federal employees hired after 1983;

- Persons employed on Jan. 1, 1984 by a non-profit organization who were mandatorily covered by Social Security on that date;

- Persons whose only pension is based on railroad employment;

- Persons whose only work in a non-Social Security-covered system was prior to 1957;

- Persons having 30 or more years of substantial earnings under Social Security.

The windfall elimination provision is quite complex. The maximum Social Security wage base, the substantial earnings factor, and the bend points referred to above change on an annual basis. Additional informa-

[13] These exemptions were taken from Social Security Administration Publication No. 05-10045, "A Pension From Work Not Covered By Social Security," (March 1991). The publication is available upon request by calling 1-800-772-1213.

tion about the applicability of this provision in a specific situation may be obtained from an agency retirement counselor, a local Social Security office, or through the toll-free Social Security telephone number (800-772-1213).

Medicare Part A

Medicare Part A is hospital insurance. It helps pay for in-patient care in a hospital, a skilled nursing facility or a hospice. It also covers such costs as regular nursing care, supplies, and operating room charges incurred while a person is hospitalized. Persons who qualify for Social Security through their own work history, through a spouse, or who have been receiving Social Security disability benefits for two years are entitled to Medicare Part A when they reach age 65.

Medicare Part A is hospital insurance and helps pay for inpatient care in a hospital.

All persons who were federal or postal employees on or after Jan. 1, 1983, are entitled to Medicare Part A when they reach age 65, even though they do not have enough quarters to qualify for Social Security benefits. For persons entitled to Social Security benefits, Part A coverage is automatic. If the person is receiving Social Security, he need do nothing. If the person is entitled to Social Security but not receiving it, he must apply for Part A to receive its benefits.

[Note: There are approximately 175,000 federal and postal annuitants who do not have any entitlement to Medicare Part A because they are neither covered by nor qualified for Social Security. Some of these individuals may be entitled to Medicare Part A through their spouse's Social Security. If a person is not entitled to Part A coverage, he may purchase it for about $3,000 annually when he reaches age 65.]

Medicare Part B

Medicare Part B (non-hospital insurance) helps pay for medically necessary physician services, out-patient hospital services, certain home health services and other medical services and supplies not covered by Part A.

Anyone aged 65 (or under age 65, disabled, and entitled to Part A) is entitled to purchase Part B coverage. The purchase of Part B is always optional. It may be purchased when an individual turns age 65 or during a Part B open season, which lasts from January 1st to March 31st each year. A person aged 65 or older may purchase Part B at any open season, but the Part B premium will be raised by 10 percent for every 12 months a person delays in enrolling in Part B after he is 65. There is no penalty, however, if a person continues to work after age 65 and is enrolled in a large group employer plan, so long as he enrolls in Part B within seven months after that job ends.

Medicare Part B is non-hospital insurance and helps pay for medical services and supplies not covered by Part A.

Health Care Considerations for Federal Retirees

For persons enrolled in FEHB and Medicare, Medicare is the primary claim payor. Its benefits are paid first and FEHB becomes a Medicare supplement.

Generally, federal retirees who enroll in Part B and an inexpensive FEHB fee-for-service plan will find that the combination produces excellent total coverage at a reasonable total premium. If an individual is enrolled in a good HMO that covers most medical care with only small co-payments (such as $5 per doctor's visit), there is probably no advantage to enrolling in Part B. If an individual plans to remain in an HMO indefinitely, Part B would not add enough to the total package of benefits to justify paying the Part B premium. If a person later switches to a fee-for-service plan, he should consider enrolling in Part B at that time.

Conclusion

Social Security and Medicare benefits provide a significant level of protection to many government employees and retirees. These benefits should be considered in any financial or estate plan.

Glossary

Administrator

The individual appointed by the probate court to oversee the administration of an estate in cases where the decedent dies intestate. An administrator's duties are nearly identical to those performed by the Executor in cases where the testator dies testate.

Administratrix

A female administrator.

Annual Gift Tax Exclusion

The maximum sum (presently $10,000) which may be given each year to an individual donee free of the imposition of gift tax liability on the donor. The annual exclusion permits a husband and wife to make tax-free gifts of $20,000 each year to an individual by means of the split gift election.

Beneficiary

A person for whose benefit a trust is created, or a person who receives a bequest or devise under a will.

Bequest

A gift of personal property, such as money or jewelry, that is left under a will.

Bypass Trust

A trust particularly useful to married couples whose total estate exceeds $600,000. In the trust, the spouse who holds the more valuable estate typically provides that up to $600,000 of his or her assets will pass into a trust for the benefit of his surviving spouse. The surviving spouse will be entitled to receive all income from the trust as well as the right to receive up to 5% of the trust principal each year. The trustee often has the discretion to make annual distributions of principal to the surviving spouse for any additional unusual expenses or medical bills. A bypass trust may also be referred to as a family trust or credit shelter trust.

Codicil

An amendment to a will which must comply with the requirements for executing a will. Codicils are typically used in instances where a testator wishes to make minor changes or amendments to a valid existing will without the expense or inconvenience of drafting an entirely new will.

Credit Shelter Trust - See Bypass Trust

Crummey Power

Non-cumulative withdrawal rights commonly provided to beneficiaries of a trust. The Crummey power permits beneficiaries to withdraw cash gifts made to a trust by the grantor for a short period of time, thereby permitting any such gifts to be considered gifts of a present interest and thus qualify for the $10,000 annual gift tax exclusion. If the withdrawal right is not exercised, it lapses and the property remains in the trust. This planning technique derives its name from the court case that held it to be permissible. The name of the taxpayer in that case was Crummey.

Decedent

A deceased person.

Devise

A gift of land or an improvement on land, such as a house, which is left under a will.

Durable Power of Attorney

See "Power of Attorney."

Estate

All property and debts left by a decedent on the date of death.

Executor

The individual who is named by a testator in his will to oversee the administration and distribution of the testator's estate after his death. Also called "Personal Representative" in some jurisdictions.

Executrix

A female executor.

Fiduciary

An individual who has a high duty of trust to act in good faith for the benefit of another. The Trustee of a Trust or Executor of an estate is a fiduciary.

Funded Trust

A trust which is funded with income-producing assets.

Grantor

The person who owns an asset which is placed in trust. Also called the "settlor" or "creator" of the trust.

Grantor Annuity Trust
> An irrevocable trust into which money or other property is transferred in exchange for an annuity of a fixed dollar amount payable to the grantor for a specified period of time.

Grantor Retained Income Trust
> A trust specifically designed to pay trust income to the grantor for a term of years with the remaining interest passing to family members at the end of any such period.

Gross Estate
> The value of all of the decedent's property on the date of death.

Guardian
> An individual who is named to oversee the well-being, health, support and educational needs of a person who is legally incompetent due to youth or physical or mental infirmity.

Inter Vivos Trust
> One created by a grantor during his life. See also Living Trust.

Intestate
> The state of dying without having executed a valid will. If a person writes a will which is declared invalid after his death, he has technically died intestate.

Intestate Succession
> State laws which govern the manner in which property is distributed upon the death of a person who dies intestate.

Irrevocable Trust
> A trust which may not be revoked or altered after it is created by the grantor. By permanently surrendering control over the property which he places in the trust, the grantor may remove all such property from his gross estate. The major advantage of structuring this type of trust is that the grantor may greatly reduce his income and estate tax liability.

Jurisdiction
> The legal system, including the laws and courts, located in a territorial zone.

Joint Tenancy with Right of Survivorship

A form of ownership which arises where two or more persons own property, usually land, whereby if one party dies, the survivor receives full title to the property

Life Insurance Trust

A trust created to buy or hold life insurance. It is generally an irrevocable trust used to permit the grantor to reduce his estate tax by transferring a life insurance policy(s) to the trust and naming the trust as owner and/or beneficiary of the policy.

Living Trust

A trust which is created and takes effect while the grantor is alive. Also called an Inter Vivos Trust.

Living Will

A document which is drafted by an individual instructing that he or she does not desire the use of life-support systems under specified circumstances. This differs from a Health Care Power of Attorney in that in the latter, the appointed agent will make decisions concerning whether medical personnel should take life-sustaining measures for the principal under given circumstances. In contrast, under a Living Will, the patient specifies that life-support systems should not be used under the circumstances set forth in the document.

Marital Deduction

An estate or gift tax deduction which permits one spouse to take an unlimited portion of another spouse's gross estate free of estate tax or gift tax.

Minor's Trust (2503(c) Trust)

A trust established for the benefit of a minor which derives its name from the section of the Internal Revenue Code which authorizes it. It permits the grantor to make a gift of a future interest to a trust established for the benefit of a minor without incurring any gift tax liability. The beneficiary must have a right to take all trust property when he reaches age 21.

Personal Representative

The individual who is named by a testator in his will to oversee the administration and distribution of the testator's estate after his death. Also called "Executor" in some states.

Pour-over

A transfer of property from an estate or trust to another estate or trust upon the occurrence of an event specified in the relevant instrument. Typically, for example, a will may designate the testator's trust as recipient of all remaining property which he owns on the date of death which is not otherwise disposed (*i.e.*, the will "pours over" into the trust).

Pour Over Trust

A trust into which assets are contributed from another source, such as the grantor's will or a source outside the estate such as life insurance proceeds.

Power of Attorney

A written instrument wherein an individual — called the "principal" — appoints another person (called the "attorney-in-fact" or "agent") to perform specified actions on his behalf due to the principal's absence or incompetency.

Durable Power of Attorney

A power of attorney in which the principal appoints another party to take certain actions on his behalf in the event he becomes mentally incompetent. In this instrument, the principal specifically states that the power will not be adversely affected or revoked in the event the principal should become incapacitated. This language is of particular significance because historically a power of attorney was automatically revoked when the principal became incapacitated, since an incompetent person lacked authority to grant binding authority to another individual.

Health Care Power of Attorney

An instrument in which the principal appoints another individual to control fundamental medical decisions which could affect his health in the event he becomes incapacitated. In many health care powers of attorney, the principal empowers the agent to direct the withholding or withdrawal of life-sustaining procedures in the event the principal becomes terminally ill. If it is properly drafted, this document should remain valid even if the principal subsequently becomes mentally incompetent.

Specific Power of Attorney

An instrument in which the principal appoints an agent as his attorney-in-fact for a limited period of time for the purpose of completing a specified task. This specific power of attorney is frequently used, for example, in connection with real estate closings where the seller or purchaser is unable to attend the closing. With the specific power of attorney, a named attorney-in-fact may sign all necessary documents on behalf of the buyer or seller.

Probate Court
The arm of the judiciary in each state which oversees the administration of decedents' estates.

QTIP Trust (Qualified Terminable Interest Trust)
A trust designed to maximize the estate tax marital deduction by providing a surviving spouse a life interest in the property without transferring outright ownership interest to a surviving spouse.

Revocable Living Trust
A trust which permits the grantor to transfer assets to a trust and change the terms of the trust during his lifetime. It either terminates at the grantor's death or it may continue in existence after the grantor dies.

Self-proving Will
A will which has been executed with rigid safeguards to minimize the risk that its validity could be successfully challenged. It is executed by the testator and the required number of witnesses in the presence of a notary public, all of whom sign a written statement which indicates that the will was executed in this manner.

Split Gift Election
See Annual Gift Tax Exclusion.

Standby Trust
A trust which is created to assume control of and manage trust assets when the grantor is no longer capable of managing his assets during his lifetime due to mental or physical disabilities.

Statutory Share
The minimal share of a decedent's estate (frequently one-half or one-third) to which a surviving spouse is entitled by operation of law regardless of the terms of the decedent's will.

Surety Bond
A legal requirement in many jurisdictions for the individual serving as executor or trustee to procure this "insurance" which will be used to reimburse beneficiaries and/or creditors in cases where a fiduciary mismanages the estate's assets.

Taxable Estate
> The property which is subject to estate tax liability after the decedent's gross estate has been reduced by all appropriate expenses and deductions. Federal estate tax liability arises only if the decedent's taxable estate exceeds $600,000.

Tenancy by the Entirety
> A form of ownership which arises where property, usually land, is owned by a husband and wife with right of survivorship. Upon the death of one spouse, the surviving spouse receives full ownership of the entire property outside the probate process. A tenancy by the entirety is particularly advantageous in that property owned as tenants by the entirety cannot be seized and sold by creditors of one spouse to satisfy any outstanding judgments unless both spouses are jointly liable to the creditor.

Testamentary Trust
> A trust which is created in the grantor's will or otherwise takes effect upon the death of the grantor.

Testate
> The state of dying after having executed a valid written will.

Testator
> A person who writes and executes a written will.

Testatrix
> A female testator.

Trust
> A form of property ownership involving three parties: the grantor, who conveys title of property to the trustee who manages it for the benefit of a third person, the beneficiary.

Trustee
> The individual or institution, such as a bank, which manages the trust property for the benefit of the trust's beneficiaries.

Trust Corpus or Trust Estate
> The property in the trust.

Unfunded Trust
    A trust which, when initially created does not have any funds, usually has as its sole asset(s) a life insurance policy, or policies, on the grantor's life.

Unified Transfer Tax Credit
    A credit available to offset federal estate or gift tax liability which permits a donor to make gifts totalling no more than $600,000 tax-free during his lifetime. Any portion remaining unused may be used to offset federal estate taxes after the donor's death.

Uniform Gifts to Minors Act (UGMA) or Uniform Transfers to Minors Act (UTMA)
    Laws passed by individual states under which money, real estate, limited partnership interest, patents, tangible personal property and other forms of property may be transferred by an adult to a minor. Gifts placed in these accounts are typically held by a trustee, or custodian, to meet future needs such as college or other expenses which may be required by the child.

Will
    A legal document which instructs how an individual's property should be distributed after his death.

ABOUT THE AUTHORS

G. Jerry Shaw was a founding partner of Shaw, Bransford and O'Rourke in 1982. He began his legal career with the Office of Chief Counsel, Internal Revenue Service (IRS), where he represented the agency in legal matters for more than 10 years. Since leaving the IRS, Shaw has focused on legal issues of interest to public employees. He helped found the Senior Executives Association (SEA), a professional association for federal senior executives, the Public Employees Roundtable (PER), a consortium of 28 federal, state and local associations that represent government managers and professional employees, and the Federal Employees Education and Assistance Fund (FEEA), a charitable and educational organization that provides benefits to federal employees, their dependents and survivors. He currently serves as General Counsel to SEA and is President of PER and FEEA. Shaw received his JD degree from St. Mary's University and has done legal post-graduate work at Georgetown University Law Center.

Thomas J. O'Rourke, who also began his legal career with the IRS, served 10 years in the Office of Chief Counsel and has been in private practice since 1983. O'Rourke has represented corporate, association, and individual clients in a variety of tax matters, including handling the lump sum litigation on behalf of a class of federal employees. He has also been involved in both domestic and international tax issues, as well as building an extensive estate practice. A graduate of Notre Dame Law School, O'Rourke holds a Master of Laws, Taxation, from the Georgetown University Law Center, served as an adjunct professor at various colleges and universities, and has published tax articles in professional journals.

FPMI PUBLICATIONS

- The Federal Manager's Guide $10.95
  to Liability (2nd Ed.)
- Managing Diversity In The *New* Reality $12.95
- The Federal Manager's Guide To EEO (3rd Ed.) . $10.95
- Supervisor's Guide to
  Federal Labor Relations (4th Ed.) $10.95
- The Ways of Wills (4th Ed.) $19.95
- The Federal Manager's Handbook (3rd Ed.) $24.95
- Managing Diversity: A Practical Guide $10.95
- A Practical Guide To Self Managed Teams $10.95
- Diversity: Straight Talk from the Trenches $10.95
- Face To Face: For Supervisors Who $12.95
  Counsel Problem Employees
- RIF and the Federal Employee (2nd Ed.) .... $ 9.95
- Customer Service in Government $10.95
- Achieving Consensus $10.95
- The Federal Manager's Guide $10.95
  To Discipline (3rd Ed.)
- EEO Settlements Through $10.95
  Interest-Based Bargaining
- Understanding The Federal .... $ 9.95
  Retirement Systems
- How To Build An Effective Team $10.95
- Improving Employee Performance (2nd Ed.) $10.95
- Career Transition: A Guide for $10.95
  Federal Employees in a Time of Turmoil
- Performance Management: Performance $10.95
  Standards and You
- Dealing With Organizational Change .... $ 6.95
- EEO Today: A Guide To Understanding .... $ 9.95
  the EEO Process
- Managing Effectively In A $12.95
  Reinvented Government (2nd Ed.)
- Managing The Civilian Workforce (2nd Ed.) $12.95
- The Bargaining Book (3rd Ed.) $12.95
- The Supervisor's Guide to .... $ 9.95
  Drug Testing (2nd Ed.)
- The Employee's Guide to Drug Testing .... $ 6.95
- Federal Manager's Guide to
  Total Quality Management .... $ 9.95
- Effective Writing for Feds .... $ 9.95
- Practical Ethics for the .... $ 9.95
  Federal Employee (2nd Ed.)
- Sexual Harassment and the .... $ 6.95
  Federal Employee (2nd Ed.)

- The Manager's Guide to Preventing .... $ 10.95
  Sexual Harassment (3rd Ed.)
- The Federal Employee's Guide to EEO .... $ 6.95
- Federal Manager's Guide to Leave .... $ 9.95
  and Attendance (3rd Ed.)
- Welcome to the Federal Government .... $ 6.95
- Using Alternative Dispute Resolution .... $ 9.95
  in the Federal Government
- A Practical Guide to Using ADR .... $ 9.95
  in the Federal Service
- RIF's and Furloughs (2nd Ed.) $14.95
- Working Together: A Practical Guide .... $ 9.95
  to Partnerships
- A Practical Guide to Interest Based Bargaining . $ 9.95
- Empowerment: A Practical Guide for Success ... $10.95
- Team Building: An Exercise in Leadership $10.95
- Managing Anger: Methods for a $10.95
  Happier and Healthier Life
- Dynamics of Diversity $10.95
- Voices of Diversity (hardback) $22.95
- 1997 Federal Personnel Guide .... $ 9.95
- Preventing Workplace Violence $10.95

PRACTITIONER PUBLICATIONS
- The Desktop Guide to Unfair Labor Practices $25.00
- The Federal Employee's Law $69.95
  Practitioners Handbook
- The Federal Practitioner's Guide $25.00
  to Negotiability
- The Union Representative's Guide to .... $ 9.95
  Federal Labor Relations (2nd Ed.)
- Permissive Bargaining and Congressional $19.95
  Intent: A Special Report

Shipping:
1-10 Books: $4;
11-50 Books: $12;
51+ Books: Actual UPS Shipping Rates

Prices Effective Through
December 31, 1997

FPMI NEWSLETTERS

The Federal Labor & Employee Relations Update
Subscription Fees   12 Months $225

The MSPB *Alert!*
Subscription Fees   12 Months $125
L&ER Update Subscribers pay only $95

The Federal EEO Update
Subscription Fees   1-9 Subscriptions
        $175 each

The Federal Manager's Edge
Subscription Fees
1-50 Subscriptions $95 each
51-100 Subscriptions $89 each
101-500 Subscriptions $82 each
501-999 Subscriptions $75 each
1000+ Subscriptions $69 each

Prices Effective
Through
December 31, 1997

ELECTRONIC NEWSLETTERS

The Electronic Edge
Subscription Fees:
1. One year subscription $295. This price includes one 3 1/2" floppy disk, one paper copy and the right to reproduce an unlimited number of copies to distribute throughout one organizational location.
2. Two year subscription: $470
3. Three year subscription: $605

The Electronic Federal Labor & Employee Relations Update
Subscription Fees
1. One subscription $595. This price includes one 3 1/2" disk, one paper copy and the right to reproduce an unlimited number of copies to distribute throughout one organizational location.
2. Two year subscription: $1,095
3. Three year subscription: $1,510

The Electronic EEO *Update*
Subscription Fees
1. One year subscription $595. This price includes one 3 1/2" disk, one paper copy and the right to reproduce an unlimited number of copies to distribute throughout one organizational location.
2. Two year subscription: $1,095
3. Three year subscription: $1,510

FPMI VIDEO TRAINING PACKAGES

• Managing Cultural Diversity
Package includes 25 guidebooks with workshops; a facilitators handbook with suggested workshop answers and a script with techniques to conduct a training session on cultural diversity; master copies of vu-graphs; and a 28 minute video on implementing cultural diversity in your agency ($295 for the complete set).

• Dealing With Misconduct
Package includes video program, 25 guidebooks ($295).

• Writing Effective Performance Standards
Package includes video program, 25 guidebooks ($295).

• Managing Under a Labor Agreement
• Managing Under the Labor Relations Law
Order separate courses for $295 each. Special package includes both video programs with 25 workbooks for each course ($495).

• Sexual Harassment: Not Government Approved
• Preventing Sexual Harassment: Some Practical Answers
Order separate courses for $295 each. Or purchase our special package of both video programs with 25 workbooks and a leader's guide ($495).

• The FAIR™ WAY To Manage Diversity
Package includes video program and 1 instructor's guide ($495).

Additional workbooks for each class are also available.
Quantity discounts are also available on all tape purchases.
Call for more information. (205) 539-1850.

FPMI TRAINING PACKAGES

• Resolving Labor Management Relations Issues Through Partnership

Includes 25 copies of the Participant's Workbook, one copy of the Instructor's Guide, 25 copies of *The Supervisor's Guide to Federal Labor Relations* and *The Union Representative's Guide to Federal Labor Relations*, plus master copies of overhead transparencies ($595).

• Practical Ethics Training for Government Managers and Employees

Includes 35 copies of the Participant's Workbook, 35 copies of *Practical Ethics for The Federal Employee*, one copy of the Instructor's Guide, and master copies of more than 50 black & white overhead transparencies ($595). Color transparencies and color slides available at additional cost.

• Effective Equal Employment Opportunity Leadership

Includes 25 copies of the Participant's Workbook, 25 copies of *The Federal Employee's Guide to EEO*, 25 copies of *The Federal Manager's Guide to EEO*, one copy of the Instructor's Guide, master copies of more than 50 black & white overhead transparencies ($595). Color transparencies and color slides available at additional cost.

Please call for more information on these packages.

Quantity discounts available.

(205) 539-1850 or fax (205) 539-0911.

FPMI SEMINARS

FPMI Communications, Inc. specializes in training seminars for federal managers and supervisors. These seminars can be conducted at your worksite at a flat rate that is substantially less than open enrollment seminars.

The instructors for FPMI seminars have all had practical experience with the federal government and know problems federal supervisors and employees face and how to deal effectively with those problems.

Some of the seminar-workshops available include:
- Building Productive Labor-Management Partnerships
- How To Use ADR and IBB
- Interest-Based Problem Solving
- Negotiating Labor Agreements Using Interest-Based Bargaining
- Negotiating Labor Agreements (Traditional)
- Pre-Retirement Seminar
- Taking Adverse and Performance-Based Actions
- Labor Relations for Supervisors
- Preventing Workplace Violence
- Resolving Organizational Conflict
- Managing the Dynamics of Organizational Change
- Making Discipline & Performance Decisions
- Managing Problem Employees Effectively
- RIF
- Developing Effective Performance Standards
- Developing Team-Based Performance Standards
- How to Review Performance with Employees
- Performance Management: New Rules, New Opportunities

- Working Together in a Diverse Workforce
- Preventing Sexual Harassment
- Effective Personnel Management for Supervisors & Managers
- How to Interview People Without Getting Fired, Demoted or Successfully Sued
- Effective Government Leadership in a Downsizing Environment
- How to Build an Effective Team in Your Agency
- Change Leadership for the '90's
- Handling ULP Disputes Effectively
- Preparing and Presenting Your Arbitration Case
- Practical Ethics and The Federal Employee
- Basic Labor Relations for Practitioners
- MSPB Advocacy
- Effective Legal Writing for Personnelists & EEO Officials
- Administrative Investigations and Report Writing
- Women in Management
- Time Management

For more information contact:
FPMI Communications, Inc.
707 Fiber Street
Huntsville, AL 35801-5833

PHONE (205) 539-1850

FAX (205) 539-0911

Email: fpmi@aol.com

Internet: http://www.fpmi.com